Berlitz

ZÁKYNTHOS & KEFALONIÁ

POCKET GUIDE

Walking Eye
mobile app

Discover the world's best destinations with the Insight Guides Walking Eye app, available to download for free in the App Store and Google Play.

The container app provides easy access to fantastic free content on events and activities taking place in your current location or chosen destination, with the possibility of booking, as well as the regularly-updated Insight Guides travel blog: Inspire Me. In addition, you can purchase curated, premium destination guides through the app, which feature local highlights, hotel, bar, restaurant and shopping listings, an A to Z of practical information and more. Or purchase and download Insight Guides eBooks straight to your device.

TOP 10 ATTRACTIONS

ÁSSOS
This picturesque coastal village sits on a charming natural harbour in Kefaloniá. See page 77.

BLUE CAVES, ZÁKYNTHOS
Swimming here is an unforgettable experience. See page 50.

VASILIKÓS PENINSULA
Beautiful beaches make this part of Zákynthos a popular location for water sports. See page 42.

ZÁKYNTHOS MUSEUM
Home to many fine icons, frescoes and carvings. See page 28.

MELISSÁNI
The magnificent cave lake is a highlight of any visit to Kefaloniá. See page 68.

MOUNT ÉNOS
Indigenous firs cover the upper reaches of Kefaloniá's highest point. See page 64.

WEST COAST ROAD OF KEFALONIÁ
Some of the most spectacular views on the island can be seen from this winding route. See page 75.

THE ARISTEON OLIVE PRESS AND MUSEUM
This is the place to learn about the olive oil production process – how it is today and how it was many years ago. See page 45.

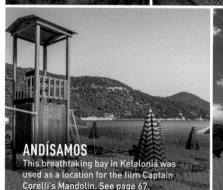

ANDÍSAMOS
This breathtaking bay in Kefaloniá was used as a location for the film Captain Corelli's Mandolin. See page 67.

WEST COAST OF ZÁKYNTHOS
A rugged and unspoilt region of traditional hill villages. See page 43.

A PERFECT TOUR OF

Day 1

Zákynthos Town

In the morning visit the Byzantine and Solomos museums and soak up the atmosphere of central Platía Solomoú, before having a light lunch at nearby Varkarola. After a siesta, stroll along the seafront for a coffee or cocktail and enjoy a fish dinner at Komis, after viewing dazzling Ágios Dionysos church.

Day 2

Boat tour of the island

Choose from one of the many boat tours that circumnavigate the island, usually in an anti-clockwise direction. This is the best way to admire the stunning coastline of Zákynthos: the two main highlights are the Blue Caves and Shipwreck Bay but look out for the Keri caves too. In the evening, dine at Malanos taverna.

Day 4

Rugged Zákynthos

Pack your bags and take a drive across the fertile plain to the rugged western mountains, visiting traditional villages, monasteries and the weaving centre at Volímes. Take a dip at the delightful little beach of Xýngi, before driving to the northern tip to Cape Skinári, to stay and eat at the unique Anemomilos converted windmills.

Day 3

Vasilikós Peninsula and Laganás Bay

Rent a car for the rest of the week, starting with a gentle drive down the Vasilikós Peninsula, stopping to visit the Sea Turtle Rescue and Information Centre at Gérakas and swim at the splendid beach. After lunch at To Triodi, head for another dip at Límni Kerioú, at the far end of Laganás Bay, before some bar action in Laganás.

ZÁKYNTHOS & KEFALONIÁ

Day 5 am

Ferry to Kefaloniá

Put the car on the morning ferry from Ágios Nikólaos to Pesáda on Kefaloniá and settle into your Argostóli hotel.

Day 7

The wild west coast

Set off early along the incredibly scenic west coast, so that you can enjoy Mýrtos beach while there is still some shade. Drop into Ássos to admire the harbour and castle, then continue north for a final swim and excellent organic meal at Odisseas in Agía Ierousalím. To avoid driving the twisting coast road at night, it's best to stay at picturesque Fiskárdo.

Day 5 pm

Southwestern Kefaloniá

In the afternoon, tour the Palliki (Lixoúri) Peninsula, swimming at beautiful Petaní beach and taking a late lunch at Ksouras. Back in the capital by evening, eat at Kyaní Akti and round the night off at Bee's Knees.

Day 6

Caves and coves

Tour along the southern coast, taking an early dip at Trapezáki, visiting the Roman mosaics at Skala and completing the loop via Póros to Sámi. After lunch at a seafront taverna, visit the famous caves of Drogaráti and Melissáni. After a late afternoon dip at the tiny cove of Agía Paraskeví, enjoy a seafood spaghetti at the eponymous taverna or drive back for a meal at To Arhontiko in Argostóli.

CONTENTS

INTRODUCTION

The close neighbours of Zákynthos and Kefaloniá do, at first glance, share a great deal: history, geographical proximity and cultural influences. However, to listen to islanders talking you would think they were as different as chalk and cheese. The Zakynthians, according to themselves, are friendly, warm and outgoing, while the Kefalonians are aloof, reserved and suspicious; the Kefalonians, for their part, claim to be proud, independent and hospitable. For all these are stereotypes, imbued with a degree of local rivalry, there is a certain truth to all of the claims.

Even at the level of the landscape, Kefaloniá is more forbidding and mountainous than green, lush Zákynthos. As for the claim that the Zakynthians are more approachable than their neighbours, it is true that the large wave of emigration and subsequent return of richer emigrés has left a much more socially and geographically fractured society on Kefaloniá than on Zákynthos.

Scented breeze

The oft-quoted Venetian saying 'Zante, Fior di Levante' (Zante, Flower of the East; see page 34) refers to the east wind that carried the perfume of the island's many wild flowers – especially the now-endangered sea daffodils – miles out to sea. The Venetian sailors could therefore smell the island before it came into sight.

GEOLOGY AND ENVIRONMENT

Another shared attribute of the islands is their important and unique natural environment. The sea around the islands is beautifully clean, crystal clear and home to two of the most endangered species to be found in Greek waters: the

Mediterranean monk seal and the Mediterranean breeding population of the loggerhead turtle.

Both islands are predominantly made of heavily folded Cretaceous limestones. Geologically they form a unit, separated from Corfu to the north by the Kefaloniá fault zone. On Zákynthos in particular the island's topography is easily related to the underlying geology. The western mountains are made of relatively hard Cretaceous limestones, while the gentler east is largely made up of Eocene deposits. The Vasilikós Peninsula is a combination of hard Triassic rocks and Plio-Pleistocene marls. Mountainous Kefaloniá largely comprises hard limestones, within which are numerous caves. The heavily folded rocks point to a turbulent geological history, and the islands' location along the Hellenic Subduction Zone gives rise to numerous earthquakes.

As well as being home to several species of mammal (including martens, *Martes foina*, and, on Kefaloniá, feral ponies) the islands have a number of interesting reptiles. One of the most spectacular is the large but harmless Aesculapian snake (*Elaphe longissima*), which can grow up to 2m (6.5ft) in length. Birds include house martins (*Delichon urbica*) and the beautiful golden oriole (*Oriolus oriolus*). Of the birds of prey, look out for the tiny Scop's owl (*Otus scops*) and the much larger buzzard (*Buteo buteo*).

TOURISM

On Zákynthos, the first package tourists arrived in 1982, brought by the British company Sunmed and later Club 18–30. This has led to indiscriminate development along the south and east coast beaches of Zákynthos, bringing in its wake a huge influx of mostly British package tourists, although numbers have plummeted in recent years due to the economic crisis. Nonetheless the boom years injected vast amounts of cash into the local economy, although much of it remains in the hands of the big international tour operators and hotel chains. Tourists also bring unwelcome social behaviour: heavy drinking, fights and the occasional more serious incident.

As well as this social disturbance, there has been a huge environmental impact from such a large number of visitors. Prior to

⊘ MYTHICAL ORIGINS

According to Greek mythology, Taphios, the son of Poseidon and Hippothoë, established the city of Taphos on the Peloponnese. Under his son Pterelaus this expanded to include the nearby Ionian islands, and so the inhabitants of Kefaloniá became known as Taphioi. The present-day name is said to come from Cephalus – a son of the king of Ileia – and the names of the four ancient cities (see page 15) from his four sons: Kranius, Paleus, Pronessos and Samos.

As for Zákynthos, Homer reported that Zakynthos was the son of King Dardanos on the Peloponnese. He settled on the island – thus giving it its name – and created the fortification of Psophidia, named after the town in Arcadia from which he came. It is possible that this was on the site of the present-day Bóhali (see page 33).

the tourist boom the island was extremely poor, with a severely underdeveloped infrastructure. Eager to exploit a steady source of income, locals threw up shoddy hotels and resorts with little regard for their environmental impact, never mind the water and sanitation needs of the visitors. By the mid-1990s it was realised that action needed to be taken to protect endangered species, such as the loggerhead turtle, and to preserve

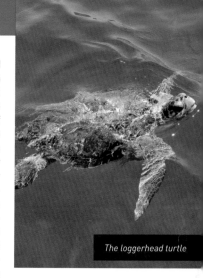

The loggerhead turtle

sensitive areas. After a long, occasionally bitter, campaign by local activists, the Marine National Park of Zákynthos was established in 1999 (see page 40). Twenty years on, there is still friction between ecologists and local businessmen and many of the protective measures that passed in law have not been implemented in practice.

The history of tourism on Kefaloniá is less invasive. It has, so far, largely escaped the ravages of mass package tourism seen in parts of Zákynthos. The relatively low-key tourist developments that do exist are mainly concentrated in Lássi on the west coast, and Skála in the south. The real boost to Kefaloniá's tourism industry came in the mid-1990s with the phenomenal success of the book *Captain Corelli's Mandolin* (see page 69). The descriptions of (pre-war) idyllic island life inspired a large number of visitors to come and see for themselves. Generally fairly affluent, these visitors (mainly from Italy and the UK) have encouraged high-end, and therefore more expensive, development. These tend to be visually kinder to

Taking it easy in Ássos

the landscape, though this has resulted in some places, Fiskárdo in particular, becoming overly twee.

ISLAND LIFE

Outside the peak months of July and August life carries on much as it does elsewhere in Greece. Many people still farm land for olives and grapes, to be harvested during the autumn and winter.

Some local tavernas, at least in the capitals, stay open throughout the winter, and this is the time when islanders tend to go out and enjoy themselves after the hard work of the tourist season. This division of the year does lead to high seasonal unemployment, and some people move to the mainland during the winter. Aside from fishing and agriculture there is little else in terms of industry on either Zákynthos or Kefaloniá – the odd quarry or small-scale food processing – but talk of trying to expand the tourist season, such as offering spring treks to see the islands' flora, has failed to be organised on a practical level.

One traditional aspect of life that endures is the singing of *kandádes* – songs performed by a group of male singers with guitar accompaniment. The music is a mix of local traditional songs, Italian popular songs and 19th-century operatic arias (a Venetian legacy). It is not unusual to hear Neapolitan favourites such as *O sole mio* in among the Greek offerings. *Arékia*, also popular, is a similar but more thoughtful solo song genre.

A BRIEF HISTORY

Evidence of early human settlement on the southern Ionian Islands is scarce. There has been little excavation of specifically palaeolithic and neolithic sites, though a number of artefacts, such as flint hand tools (for example scrapers) have been found, some of which are on display in Argostóli's archaeological museum. The earliest human presence is thought to date from the mid-Palaeolithic era (c.50,000 years ago), when, due to ice-age reduction in sea levels, the Ionians were joined to present-day Greece and Italy. It is thought that hunting groups arrived in the region, probably searching for food, from the Píndos (northern Greece) and the Peloponnese. These groups then settled on what are now the islands of Zákynthos and Kefaloniá.

THE BRONZE AGE

Archaeologists now know that there was a thriving Mycenean society on Kefaloniá. As yet, aside from the Bronze-Age tombs close to Kambí on the west coast, there is little corresponding evidence from Zákynthos. It is assumed, backed up by artefacts found during excavations, that the four city-states of ancient Kefaloniá (see box) have their origins in the Late-Helladic period of c.1500–1050 BC. One of the major centres on Kefaloniá appears to have been near Tzanáta in the southeast, about 8km (5 miles) from the site of Pronnoi, of interest

> ### Four city-states
>
> Ancient Kefaloniá was a Tetrapolis, comprised of four independent city-states. These were: Pali on present-day Pallíki, Krani near Drápano, Sámi near the port of the same name, and Pronnoi in the south of the island.

The Mycenean tholos tomb near Tzanáta, Kefaloniá

due to its possible links to Odysseus. Other important sites on Kefaloniá include: the chamber tombs at Mazarakáta, first excavated by C.P. de Bosset in 1813; the Late-Helladic chamber tombs at Metaxáta; and the Late-Helladic chamber tomb at Lakíthra, which yielded the richest finds of any of the island's Bronze-Age tombs.

THE ARCHAIC, CLASSICAL AND HELLENIC PERIODS

The origins of the city-states of Kefaloniá and the early rulers of Zákynthos are the subjects of Greek mythology (see page 12). However, there are more recent historical references; Zákynthos and the four city-states of Kefaloniá were mentioned by both Herodotus and Thucydides. Zákynthos seems to have been an independent region, ruled by leaders who originally came from the Peloponnese, possibly nearby Achaia. This independence lasted until just before the outbreak of the

Peloponnesian War (431 BC), when the island was conquered by the Athenian general Tolmides; it was hence on the side of Athens during most of the conflict.

The pattern on Kefaloniá was more complex. The city-states were generally politically independent of each other and formed their own alliances; Pali alone fought in the Persian Wars, at the battle of Plataea (479 BC). However, up until the Peloponnesian War they were all to a greater or lesser extent – but particularly Pali – allied to Corinth. Krani also had links to the Athenians and, on the outbreak of the Peloponnesian War, the whole island was brought under the sphere of Athens.

At some point during the archaic and Classical periods (from c.750 BC) the Kefalonian city-states became demo-cratic. Professor G. Moschopoulos notes that the Kefalonian *demos* (citizens eligible to vote – this excluded women and slaves) took part in political decision-making, and that the *vouli* (the city parliament) was the 'dominant institution' in the city of Pali. He also points out that none of the coins from the

⊘ ODYSSEUS

The Homeric epic *The Odyssey* follows the adventures of its eponymous hero from Troy, on the coast of Anatolia, back home to mythical Ithaca. For a long time it was assumed that Ithaca was present-day Itháki and numerous local features were named after events in the epic. However, there is no archaeo-logical evidence to back these claims and the latest thinking points to southern Kefaloniá as the most likely spot for the king-dom. Zákynthos is completely out of the running, although it is mentioned by name in both *The Odyssey* and *The Iliad*.

city-states showed an image of a ruler (except for that of the mythical founder Cephalus; see page 12).

Towards the end of the Peloponnesian War Zákynthos fell under the sphere of Sparta, while the Kefalonian cities wavered in their allegiance between Sparta and Athens, and in 226 BC became a member of the Aetolic marine confederation. Later, both islands came to the attention of the Macedonians. Philip V occupied Zákynthos – and temporarily lost the island to the Romans during the 2nd Punic War (218–202 BC) – but failed to conquer Kefaloniá. The end of Hellenistic influence came when the Romans, under Marcus Fulvius Nobili, conquered Zákynthos in 191 BC and Kefaloniá in 189 BC.

THE BYZANTINES AND FRANKS

From the point of the Roman invasion to the advent of Byzantine rule in 337 AD little of note is recorded in the history of either island. However, the archaeological record shows a certain degree of wealth and artistic activity, as at the villa at Skála on Kefaloniá (see page 64). Under the Byzantines the islands, Kefaloniá in particular, became active in defending the empire against attack from Arab pirates, and, in 850, Kefaloniá became the head of a *thema*, or administrative district. Zákynthos fared less well during this period, and the sacking of the island by the Vandals in 474 was the first of a number of attacks by outside forces.

As the power of the Byzantines waned, attacks on both islands became more common. In 1085 Robert Guiscard, a Norman leader, attacked Fiskárdo on Kefaloniá, and by 1185 the island was under the rule of the Franks (a disparate group of largely Norman and Italian fiefdoms). In 1204, after the sacking of Constantinople during the infamous Fourth Crusade, Zákynthos followed suit and remained under Frankish rule until 1479. The Frankish rulers of Kefaloniá were a diverse group, at first headed by the Venetian Orsini family, to whom it passed after the Fourth Crusade. In 1357 it was passed, by the King of Naples, to the Tocco family, the most remarkable member of which was Francesca, wife of Carlo I, who reigned after his death, setting up a court of women in Kástro Agíou Georgíou (see page 59).

THE OTTOMANS AND VENETIANS

With the growing power of the Ottoman Turks to the east, it was inevitable that the islands would soon receive their attention, and, in 1479, Zákynthos and Kefaloniá were attacked by Ahmad Pasha. The Ottomans overran the islands, taking many prisoners back to Istanbul. Although the Venetians, then the other major force in the eastern Mediterranean, regained Kefaloniá in 1481, it was ceded back to Sultan Beyazit II in a treaty in 1485.

The Venetian fort at Ássos, Kefaloniá

The Venetians were not deterred from ideas of Mediterranean domination, however, and in 1489 invaded and took over control of Zákynthos. Eleven years later, in 1500, they attacked Kefaloniá with the help of a Spanish army, and, after a two-month siege, took control of Kástro Agíou Georgíou on Christmas Day. Thus, apart from a brief period, the islands are among the few areas of Greece not to have come under Ottoman rule or been noticeably influenced by it.

The two islands remained under the Venetians until 1797. This was a period of relative calm, although the Venetians ensured that both Zákynthos and Kefaloniá were heavily defended; the impressive castles at Bóhali on Zákynthos, and Ássos and Agíou Geórgiou (the long-time Venetian capital) on Kefaloniá are a legacy of Venetian rule. Not only were the islands prized as staging posts for the Venetian navy, they were also useful for their agricultural production and most of the many olive trees now seen on the islands were planted during this time.

One of the most visible legacies of the Venetian occupation is the large number of splendid churches, many with ornate, gilded baroque interiors, found on the islands. Much of the churches' interior decoration and many of their icons, is the work of Cretan sculptors and painters, who fled to Zákynthos and Kefaloniá after Crete fell to the Ottomans in 1669. Once on the two Ionian islands, they came under the influence of the Italian Renaissance and the resulting artistic

Earthquake zone

'The reason they build their houses so lowe [on Zákynthos] is because of the manifold Earthquakes which doe as much share this Iland as any other place in the World.'
Thomas Coryat, 1612

synthesis is known as Ionian School painting.

The local rulers came from Venetian aristocratic families, who acquired large estates and settled on the islands. Their names were inscribed in what was called the *Libro d'Oro* (Golden Book). With the greater exposure to the Western world, a number of schools, mostly for religious instruction, were established, bringing the teachings of the enlightenment to the islands. For all this, they were still under autocratic rule and people were not immune from the rumblings of nationalist discontent that grew steadily in the 18th century.

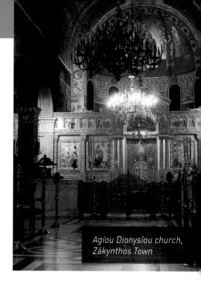

Agíou Dionysíou church, Zákynthos Town

THE SEPTINSULAR REPUBLIC AND THE BRITISH

This discontent became evident when, in 1797, the islands were occupied by the revolutionary French. The heartening revolutionary fervour with which the islanders greeted the invaders – the *Libro d'Oro* was burnt in Argostóli's main square – initially went into radical proposals such as the abolition of religion. However, the rival powers, specifically the Orthodox Russians, were unhappy about Napoleon's widening sphere of influence and agitation against the French began to ferment. In 1798 a joint Russian and Turkish fleet sailed for the islands and, with local support, they fell easily to the invaders.

The subsequent Treaty of Constantinople, signed in 1800, ushered in the creation of an autonomous republic under Turkish suzerainty. This, the Eptánisos Politía (or Septinsular Republic), became the first, nominally, independent modern Greek state. Not all went smoothly, however, particularly on Kefaloniá, where Argostóli and Lixoúri were engaged in bitter, sometimes violent, rivalry for political dominance.

The fledgling state came to an end in 1807, when the islands passed back to the French under the Treaty of Tilsit, and in turn Zákynthos and Kefaloniá were occupied by the British in 1809. The British occupation, which lasted until 1863, was not an entirely happy time for the islanders. Although the British did carry out a number of public works (such as building the Ágios Georgíos lighthouse and Drápano bridge near Argostóli), the local population became increasingly unhappy about foreign occupation and rule, especially after the creation of the neighbouring modern Greek state in 1828–32. Although the largely complicit urban middle class had a comfortable standard of living, the peasant farmers were oppressed and poor and, on Kefaloniá in 1848–9, they staged two armed revolts against British rule.

INDEPENDENCE

The two islands had long been a place of refuge for independence fighters from the mainland (the military leader Kolokotronis had landed on Zákynthos in 1805), and in 1863 the islanders' nationalist ambitions were finally realised when the London Protocol declared the Ionian islands part of Greece.

The enlightenment ideals that had spurred the islanders to agitate for independence manifested themselves post-1863 in radical politics. Kefaloniá in particular was a hotbed of dissent and was the home of Marinos Antypas, the 'first Greek socialist', who was murdered in Thessaly in 1907. A more disturbing side of this penchant for radicalism came through in the fascist dictator Ioannnis Metaxas, a native of Kefaloniá, who ruled Greece from a military coup in 1936 until his death in 1941, two months before the German invasion of Greece.

WORLD WAR II AND THE 1953 EARTHQUAKE

The next 15 years or so were a period of great hardship for the islands, resulting in a large number of families leaving for Australia, the US and South Africa. The first catastrophe was World War II. Although the Greeks initially repulsed and held Mussolini's forces in 1940–41, more powerful joint Axis forces overran the country during 1941. Zákynthos and Kefaloniá were initially under the Italians but when Italy capitulated

in 1943 the Germans invaded, imposed a more brutal regime and, on Kefaloniá, executed most of the Italian soldiers (as told in *Captain Corelli's Mandolin*, see page 69).

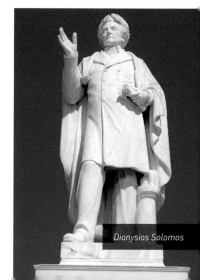

The islands had just begun to recover from the joint effects of World War II and the ensuing Greek Civil War when, in August 1953, they were struck by a huge earthquake. The epicentre was on the seabed between Zákynthos and Kefaloniá, so the impact was felt more in

Dionysios Solomos

the southern, settled parts of Kefaloniá, and the northern part of Zákynthos, which was relatively unpopulated. The devastation on Kefaloniá was almost total and over 400 people were killed. Zákynthos Town was also completely destroyed, not only by the quake itself but also by fire and explosions, due in part to cooking fires and the illegal practice of keeping a box of dynamite under the bed to help with illicit fishing.

THE ARRIVAL OF TOURISM

Many people from the richer island of Kefaloniá emigrated. Far fewer left Zákynthos, which in particular suffered a period of great poverty that only began to lift when, in 1982, the first package tourists arrived. This sparked a wave of indiscriminate tourist development, spreading like a rash along the sandy beaches of the south and east coasts. Kefaloniá was relatively ignored until the phenomenal success of *Captain Corelli's Mandolin* brought tourists to the island in the 1990s, at the same time as emigré Kefalonians began to return from abroad. The environmental dangers of tourism have become more than evident, and, ironically, it may be the downturn in tourism that saves the day rather than the proposed green measures.

Mýrtos Beach, Kefaloniá

HISTORICAL LANDMARKS

c.50,000 BC Evidence of Palaeolithic settlement.

c.1500–1050 BC Establishment of the four city states of Kefaloniá.

191–189 BC Conquest of the islands by the Romans.

AD 337 The islands come under Byzantine rule.

1185–1479 Frankish occupation of the islands.

1479 Ottomans overrun the islands, taking many locals prisoner.

1489–1500 The Ottomans are driven from the islands (Zákynthos: 1489; Kefaloniá: 1500) by Venetians, never to return. This ensures that the islands are among the few areas of Greece to remain free of Ottoman control and influence.

1500–1797 Era of Venetian rule leads to the appearance of distinctive churches and olive plantations.

1797 The islands are occupied by the revolutionary French.

1798 Russians and Turks, unhappy at Napoleon's widening influence, mount a joint expedition and take the islands from the French.

1800 Treaty of Constantinople. The Eptánisos Politía becomes the first autonomous modern Greek state, albeit under Turkish suzerainty.

1807 Treaty of Tilsit. The islands pass back to the French.

1809–63 British occupation of the islands.

1848–9 Two armed revolts against British rule by peasant farmers.

1863 The London Protocol declares the Ionian Islands part of Greece.

1941–3 World War II. Greece is occupied initially by Italians, then Germans.

1953 A huge earthquake hits Kefaloniá and Zákynthos, destroying almost all buildings and killing over 400 people.

1982 First package tours arrive on Zákynthos.

1999 National Marine Park of Zákynthos is established.

2000 Captain Corelli's Mandolin, starring Penélope Cruz and Nicholas Cage, is filmed on Kefaloniá.

2014 Alexis Tsipras, of the far left Syriza Party, becomes Greece's prime minister but austerity continues.

2016 Greece agrees a financial breakthrough deal with its creditors.

2019 Centre-right New Democracy wins the July elections, led by Kyriakos Mitsotakis.

Iconic Navágio Bay, Zákynthos

WHERE TO GO

ZÁKYNTHOS

Zákynthos, also known by its Italian name Zante, is the southernmost of the Ionian islands that lie off the western coast of mainland Greece. The island divides into three geographical areas: the Vasilikós Peninsula in the southeast, a central plain, and the wild and mountainous north and west. One of the greenest of all the Greek islands, it has good, fertile soil and receives a generous amount of rain in the winter and early spring.

Although Zákynthos is now thoroughly Greek, evidence of the island's Venetian heritage is inescapable, from its Italianate church towers to the descendants of aristocratic Venetian families, still major landowners.

ZÁKYNTHOS TOWN

The once-elegant harbour town of **Zákynthos ❶** had its public buildings and squares rebuilt approximately as they were before the 1953 earthquake, but in reinforced concrete. Ferries from Kyllíni pull in at the long jetty at the southern end of the harbour, where the port authority can also be found.

Running parallel to the harbour is the main shopping street of Alex. Románou where you will find most of the upmarket boutiques and jewellers. Románou ends at Platía Agíou Márkou, which adjoins Platía Solomoú, the focus of the northern end of the harbourfront, around which the town's museums and municipal buildings are clustered.

The Byzantine Museum of Zákynthos

On Platía Solomoú is the **Byzantine Museum of Zákynthos** Ⓐ (www.zanteisland.com; Tue–Sun 8.30am–3pm), also known simply as the Zákynthos Museum. It contains many pieces from the old Pandokrátora Museum, as well as frescoes, icons and carvings rescued from churches devastated in the 1953 earthquake. There are also 17th- to 19th-century religious paintings of the Ionian School, founded by Cretan artists fleeing the Ottoman conquest who met local artists strongly influenced by the Italian Renaissance.

Start in the room on your right as you go in. Here you will find a wonderful carved iconostasis by Angelos Mosketis (1683). This was rescued from the church of Pandokrátora (1517), and alongside are photos of the damage to the church caused by the earthquake, and of its reconstruction. The other impressive iconostasis at the end of the room dates from 1690 and is from Agíou Dimítrios tou Kóla (both churches are in Zákynthos Town). There is also a splendid icon of the Virgin from the same church.

As you climb the stairs to the first floor there is a room off to the left, full of icons. A number of these, on the right, came from the old museum. There are some very fine Venetian-inspired paintings from Agías Ekaterínis tou Grypári in Zákynthos Town, and 16th-century icons from Agíou Pnévmatos in Gaïtáni. Perhaps the most interesting work here is the 17th-century representation of Jerusalem from Agías Ekaterínis ton Kípon,

Two-faced island

While Zákynthos's beautiful sandy beaches, concentrated on its southern and eastern coasts, are popular with package holidaymakers, the rest of the island – especially the west coast – remains rugged and, for the most part, undeveloped.

Zákynthos Town harbourfront

Zákynthos Town. Look closely and you will see that this is a very Christian representation of the holy city, with no evidence of its Muslim heritage to be seen.

On the first floor you begin in a small room which contains carved Byzantine stonework (10th- to 11th-century), one piece of which shows the Byzantine double-headed eagle. Then you enter what is possibly the museum's star exhibit, the fabulous, fully frescoed interior of the monastery church of Agíou Andréa in Mesovoúni Volimón. The church itself is 16th century, while the paintings date from the 17th century. The frescoed interior is set out as it was in situ and a number of precious sacred vessels are laid out in front of the apse.

There follows a long corridor with a display of silver censers. The first bay contains rescued frescoes from Agíou Georgíou ton Kalogrión (1669); there are also two panels, one of St Nicholas and one of two angels with a scroll, from Agías Ánnas (1715). The

A 17th-century Ionian School icon in the Zákynthos Museum

second bay has a superb series of icons rescued from across the island. Particularly notable are the Panagía i Amólyndos from Agíou Nikólaou tou Mólou, the 17th-century Ágios Ioánnis o Hrysóstomos from Agíou Ioánni tou Tráfou, and the 17th-century Ascension of the Virgin from the old museum.

The next bay holds late 17th- to 18th-century icons, including a splendid 18th-century one of Jonah and the Whale from Agíou Spyrídona tou Flabouriári. The final bay is given over to 12 baroque paintings from the iconostasis of Agíon Anargýron by Nikolaos Koutouzis (1741–1813) and Nikolaos Kantounis (1767–1834). On the way down the stairs, on the left, are Kantounis' paintings from Agíou Georgíou ton Kalogrión.

The final room, on the ground floor, houses a notable model of Zákynthos Town before the 1953 earthquake, giving a good idea of its attractive Italianate character before it was destroyed. On the walls are paintings by Koutzouzis from the church of Agíou Spyrídona tou Flabouriári.

The Library

Next to the town's theatre, also on Platía Solomoú, is the **Library** (winter Mon–Wed noon–7pm, Thu–Sat 8.30am–1pm, summer Mon–Sat 8.30am–1pm), where there is a small display of photographs showing the island pre-1953. As well as views of the town and the lavish interiors of some of the island's churches, there are photos of the elegant interiors of the mansions of the Zakynthian Italian aristocracy, in particular those of the now destroyed town palace of the locally prominent Komoutou family. At the top of the stairs is a small room with a rather bizarre collection of dolls in what purports to be traditional Zakynthian dress (strictly speaking there is no such thing).

Close to the Library, on the corner of the square by the sea, is the reconstructed church of **Agíou Nikólaou tou Mólou**. The attractive stone building is worth a quick visit. However, many of its original icons are now housed in the nearby Byzantine Museum of Zákynthos.

The Solomos Museum

Set back from Platía Solomoú is Platía Agíou Márkou, with a number of cafés, on the far side of which is the **Museum of Dionysios Solomos and Andreas Kalvos B** (www.zanteisland. com; daily 9am–2pm). Named after Greece's national poet, the museum is dedicated to famous Zakynthians – these are noticeably male, and in most cases, famous in local terms only. Inside, on the left, are the rather grand tombs of Solomos and Andreas Kalvos, a fellow poet (see box).

The main body of the museum lies upstairs. The room in front of you is dedicated to the fine icon collection of Nikolaos and Thaleia Kolyvos. On the right is a room containing set and costume designs for productions of the work of the playwright Dionysios Romas. The gallery

Home to rest

In 1960 the bodies of Andreas Kalvos and his English wife were brought to Zákynthos from Keddington, in Lincolnshire, where the poet had spent much of his life.

given over to exhibits on Solomos himself (writer of the lyrics of the Greek national anthem and a champion of Demotic Greek) has a number of portraits, samples of his handwriting and, more bizarrely, a glass urn containing earth from his first grave in Corfu. Visitors might be surprised to notice that many of the manuscripts are in Italian, his first language. It was only with his rising nationalist consciousness that he turned to writing in Greek.

Further on, there is an interesting case containing memorabilia of the operetta composer and musician Pavlos Karreri (1829–96), otherwise known as Paul Carrer. Close by, there is an imposing coloured lithograph of *The Great Battle of 'Garibaldin' at Siatista under the Leadership of Alexandros Romas'*, next to which is a portrait of Romas himself, looking disturbingly like Joseph Stalin.

Moní Agíou Dionysíou

On the seafront, at the southern end of the harbour, is the most important church of Zákynthos town, **Agíou Dionysíou** Ⓒ (daily 8am–1pm, 5–10pm). It was founded by monks living in seclusion on one of the islands of Strofádes (80km/50 miles south of Zákynthos), where they had been guarding the body of the Zakynthian Ágios Dionýsios. In 1717, to escape the attacks of pirates, they brought the body to Zákynthos and re-established their monastery. In 1764 the church was remodelled, and a bell tower built beside it in 1854. However, the church was completely destroyed in an earthquake in 1893. The present church – an earthquake-proof building – was completed in 1948 and was one of the very few buildings to survive the 1953 earthquake.

The church's interior, although modern, is well worth a look. Every inch is covered with paintings and gilding. Around the church, over the tops of the pillars, are a series of panels describing the exploits of the saint, as well as of the relic of his body. One

Zákynthos Town from Bóhali Castle

of the more bizarre episodes shows the monks using the desiccated body of the saint to expel a plague of locusts. On the right-hand side of the nave is a small chapel containing the grave of the saint. The impressive silver coffin was made in 1829 by Diamantis Bafas. He also made the silver surrounds for the icons on the church's intricately carved wooden iconostasis. The saint has two festival days, celebrated on 24 August and 17 December.

Bóhali Froúrio

Above the town in the Bóhali district, is the huge Venetian **Froúrio ⓓ**, or fort (June–Sep daily 8am–8pm; Oct–May Tue–Sun 8.30am–3pm). Thought to stand on the site of ancient Psophida, the fortress has Byzantine antecedents, but any traces of these earlier settlements – with the exception of the 12th-century church of the Pandokrátor – have been destroyed by earthquakes. The present fortifications were built under the Venetian

Proveditor general da mar Giovanni Battisto Grimani and finished in 1646. As a prime defensive site, the fort served as a place of refuge for local people and, particularly in the 17th century, became a flourishing settlement. The fort fell into disuse in 1864, when Zákynthos became part of the Greek Republic.

The Froúrio lies at the end of a winding road that leads up from the town through Bóhali village. Just before the top of the hill is the village *platía* in front of the church, with a few cafés and tavernas that have a lovely view over Zákynthos Town and harbour. The inside of the fort is now a beautiful pine wood, and you have to search around for the remains of the buildings (there is a useful site plan at the entrance). However, perhaps the main reason for coming up to the Froúrio is the spectacular panoramic view. The

⊙ SONNET – TO ZANTE

Fair isle, that from the fairest of all flowers,
Thy gentlest of all gentle names dost take!
How many memories of what radiant hours
At sight of thee and thine at once awake!
How many scenes of what departed bliss!
How many thoughts of what entombéd hopes!
How many visions of a maiden that is
No more – no more upon thy verdant slopes!
No more! Alas, that magical sad sound
Transforming all! Thy charms shall please no more –
Thy memory no more! Acccurséd ground
Henceforth I hold thy flower-enamelled shore,
O hyacinthine isle! O purple Zante!
'Isola d'oro! Fior di Levante!'
Edgar Allan Poe, 1837

site's slow renovation by the EU and Greek Ministry of Culture has ground to a halt and shorter opening hours mean sunsets must be enjoyed from the cafés below.

On the way up Bóhali hill, on the left-hand side coming from town, is the **Milanio Nautical Museum** (tel: 26950 42436 for opening hours). The work of one man, the museum tells the history of Greek seafaring through a series of model boats, as well as an eclectic assortment of naval artefacts.

Vines are intensively cultivated in these parts

CENTRAL PLAIN

The island's central plain is the most fertile in the Ionian Islands. It is mostly given over to the intensive cultivation of vines and, away from the resorts and airport, is sprinkled with attractive little villages. Separating the plain from the eastern coast is a line of steep but low hills, and on the western side the mountains rise sharply and dramatically. Along the foot of mountains lie a string of villages, many located at points where springs emerge from the hills above.

The central villages include sleepy little Gaïtáni with an attractive Italianate church, and a characteristic separate bell tower, which dates from 1906. Similar architecture can be seen in neighbouring tiny settlements of Vanáto and Hourhoulídi. The detached bell towers seen across the island are built away from the church to prevent the bells falling through its roof in the event of an earthquake.

On the road between Zákynthos Town and Maherádo is the **Oenolpi Winery** (www.oenolpi.gr). There has been a vineyard belonging to the Christoforos family on this spot since 1965 but when the Oenolpi Company was established in 2000, a new modern factory was built that produces some of the best wines on the island. Visitors are invited to tour the estate and the factory, and, of course, to taste the wines.

Maherádo, Agía Marína and Pigadákia

At the foot of the steep climb up to Kiliómeno is the large village of **Maherádo**, home to a couple of interesting churches and some surviving, albeit decaying, examples of traditional pre-earthquake architecture. The village square by the church of Agías Mávras has two nearby cafés serving basic food such as *souvláki*, salad and *tzatzíki*.

The main sight in Maherádo was the pilgrimage church of **Agías Mávras**. The icon of Agía Mávra was supposedly found on this spot and a church built around it. However, a devastating fire in 2005 destroyed the roof and much of the baroque interior by Nikolaos Latsis. Some of the contents were saved and it is still in the process of being restored. The festival of Agía Mávra, who is said to help healing, is celebrated at the beginning of June.

On the left-hand side, just after turning up the hill towards Kiliómeno, is a modern convent whose church has an attractively painted interior. Wrap-around skirts are provided for visitors whose dress is not modest enough for a church visit.

North of Maherádo, and higher up the mountainside, is the village of **Agía Marína**. The eponymous church has an impressive interior but is often locked. Also here is the **Hélmi Museum**

of Natural History (www.
museumhelmis.gr; May–
Oct daily 9am–5pm, Nov–
Apr 9am–2pm), with a
small but informative display on the flora and fauna
of the island.

Further on is **Pigadá-
kia ❷**, named after its
springs (*pigí* in Greek). The
lovely 16th-century church
of **Agíou Pandelímona** has
a holy spring in the saint's
shrine under the altar,
said to promote heal-
ing; this is one of the few

Hilltop church, Gerakári

places where you can go behind the iconostasis. The traditional
papadosiakoús dance is performed at the saint's festival on 27
July. The **Vertzagio Museum** (Mar–Oct daily 9am–2pm & Sun–
Fri 6–8pm) here has a motley display of rural artefacts.

Gerakári, Kypséli and Tragáki

Three pretty hilltop villages sit on the slopes in the north of the
plain. They are **Gerakári**, **Kypséli** and **Tragáki**, the southernmost, largest and most strung out. They all give splendid views
over the plain below. One of the few places to eat in Tragáki is
the Amboula tavern.

Just 5km (3 miles) southeast of Tragáki, in Sarakinádo, is
the **Zante Water Village** (www.zantewatervillage.gr; May–Oct
hours vary), which is a great family day out. The park includes
a variety of waterslides, swimming pools, Jacuzzis, and even
has a go-kart circuit.

The east coast

Leaving Zákynthos Town heading north, you pass through **Kryonéri**, along the seafront. The water is reasonably clean, especially given its proximity to the harbour, and the locals swim off the rocks and narrow pebbly beach here. After the steep climb up to pleasant, strung-out Akrotíri, the road runs inland along the ridge before descending back down to the sea at **Tsiliví**. This is the first of a string of resorts and not the most pleasant. Situated on a lovely bay with a decent beach, Tsiliví is dominated by loud bars, shops peddling tourist souvenirs and holidaymakers going red in the sun. Tsiliví blends seamlessly into Plános before things quieten down a bit at Boúka.

After the small promontory of Akrotírio Gáidaros, for the next 4km (2.5 miles) between Aboúla and Amoúdi, the road passes turn-offs to a string of small, quiet beaches. There are rooms to rent at most of them, and there are a couple of excellent beachside tavernas. About 1km (0.6 miles) beyond Amoúdi is **Alikaná**, perhaps the most pleasant of the resorts along this coast. Towards the sea it is still fairly quiet and the mountain backdrop is lovely.

At the northernmost point of the Central Plain is the large resort of **Alykés**. A larger version of Tsiliví, Alykés has all the facilities expected of a Greek package resort – cheap accommodation, all-day English breakfasts and football on satellite TV. It is, however, on a sweeping bay with a sandy beach and views of Kefaloniá. The exposed bay attracts windsurfers and can produce some surf. This is also one of the places you can take a boat to the Blue Caves near Skinári (trips are advertised everywhere; see page 50). Behind the town are the old saltworks, the large pans forming shallow lakes where salt was obtained from seawater through evaporation. These are now no longer used, as it

Laganás

is cheaper to import salt from the mainland. Consequently, the stagnant water can be rather smelly.

LAGANÁS BAY

If you dislike mass tourism and loud nightclubs, the place you will most want to avoid on Zákynthos is **Laganás**. Ironically, this, the island's most notorious resort, is right in the middle of its most environmentally sensitive area. It is estimated that these days Zákynthos receives up to 500,000 visitors every year, half of whom stay in Laganás on the south coast. They come for the wonderful sandy beach that stretches from the Vasilikós Peninsula in the east to Límni Kerioú beach in the west. This lively nightspot – or den of iniquity, depending on your point of view – is brash, noisy and nocturnal. Apart from its crowded beach, the resort's main attraction is its nightlife; one of the more popular spots is on the island of Ágios Sóstis, joined to the shore by a walkway. **Kalamáki**, 4km (2.5 miles) east of Laganás, is perhaps the most pleasant of the hectic resorts on this side of the bay.

National marine park

In response to these conflicting demands on the bay – and after intense campaigning by local environmentalists – in 1999 the Greek government established the **National Marine Park of Zákynthos ❸**, the country's first. The protected area takes in: the marine area and beaches of Laganás Bay, and around capes

⊙ NATIONAL PARK RULES

Within the confines of the national park, you must not:
fish
light a fire
camp
pick any plants
throw away ANY rubbish
On turtle nesting beaches there is:
no access between sunset and sunrise
no use of umbrellas 5m (16ft) from the waterline
no digging in the sand
no disturbing the cages protecting the nests
no use of any vehicle
no access for horses
no access for dogs without a leash
no use of ANY lights at night
Access and speed is restricted for boats across the whole area. The strictly protected area around Sekánia has access only for scientists with permission.

Marathiá and Yérakas at either end; an area of land stretching back from the beach, and behind that a buffer zone that extends almost as far as Zákynthos Town; and the Strofádes Islands 80km (50 miles) to the south. The park's effectiveness has periodically been compromised due to frequent funding shortages that often leave it unstaffed and unprotected. Thankfully the crusading Gérakas Sea Turtle Rescue and Information Centre (see page 43) monitors the situation.

The walkway to Ágios Sóstis

However, the entire bay is the most important nesting site for the loggerhead turtle *(Caretta caretta)* in the Mediterranean basin. The turtles are very sensitive to human disturbance and have suffered greatly from the indiscriminate development of this coast.

The turtles roam throughout the Mediterranean (there is evidence to suggest they use the Gulf of Gabés off Tunisia as a wintering ground) and in the spring return to Laganás Bay to nest. They rest and mate in the bay while waiting to come ashore during the night. After nightfall, the females crawl up the beach to find a suitable nesting site in the soft sand; if they are disturbed by noises or lights they will return to the sea without laying any eggs. If they are not disturbed, they dig a deep hole and lay a clutch of about 120 eggs. These take about two months to hatch, after which the hatchlings dig their way to surface and – at night – make their way down to the sea.

Conflicts with humans arise not only due to pressures of space, forcing the turtles on to fewer beaches and raising the nesting density, but particularly due to disturbance of the nests themselves and, once the turtles have emerged from their shells, from light pollution. The hatchlings find their way to the sea using reflected starlight on the water. Any shoreside lighting confuses the tiny turtles, causing them to make their way inland, where they will die.

The park is home not only to the famous turtles but also the critically endangered Mediterranean monk seal (11–12 of which inhabit sea caves outside of the park), and is important as a rest stop for migrating birds. It also protects certain species of plants, particularly the sea daffodil (*Pancratium maritimum*) and the seabed cover of Posidonia (*Posidonia oceania*), which contributes a large part of the oxygen in the Mediterranean. The habitat of **Lake Kerí** (Límni Kerioú) is the last remaining wetland of Zákynthos, important for migrating bird species. There used to be a huge lake behind Laganás that stretched almost as far as Zákynthos Town, but this was drained to make way for the airport.

The Vasilikós Peninsula

On the eastern side of Laganás Bay is one of the most beautiful parts of the island, the **Vasilikós Peninsula**. Heading south from Zákynthos Town the first place you come to is the resort of Argási, which has suffered more than most places from the tourism decline. As the land starts to rise, things begin to improve. Set against the backdrop of Mount Skopós, there are a string of beautiful small beaches along the northern edge of the peninsula. The longest of these, Paralía Iónio, is near the strung-out village of Vasilikós. Iónio runs into the nudist Banana Beach, and around the cape from here is the popular water sports centre at **Ágios Nikoláos**. On the opposite side of the bay is the unsympathetic development at Pórto Róma.

The best beach, however, is on the southwestern side at **Gérakas** ❹, a superb sweep of sand fringed by cliffs. There is only one problem – this corner of paradise is an important nesting site for turtles. Access is controlled by a park ranger en route to the beach, and numbers are limited to protect the nests. For those who want to get even closer to nature, the far end of the beach is nudist.

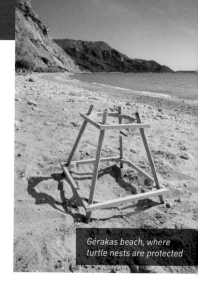
Gérakas beach, where turtle nests are protected

The exemplary **Gérakas Sea Turtle Rescue and Information Centre**, run by the environmental organisation Earth, Sea and Sky (www.facebook.com/earthseasky.ioniannatureconserva tion), provides information on the turtles and the other flora and fauna of the peninsula. They can also advise on joining volunteer environmental protection programmes (see page 89).

Further back up the peninsula's west coast is the isolated beach of Dáfni, with a pleasant *psarotavérna*, reached by a very rough road from Vasilikós. Between Dáfni and Kalamaki is the totally protected beach of Sekánia (access is only given to scientists with prior permission).

THE HILL VILLAGES AND WEST COAST

The wild and mountainous west coast is the least-spoilt part of the island, with hillsides covered in bright green *maquis* and small, dry-stone-walled fields. The land falls to the sea

The cliffs at Cape Kerí

in precipitous cliffs, with no easily accessible beaches; one reason why it has so far resisted tourist development. The sea caves at the foot of the cliffs are used for breeding by the very few remaining pairs of Mediterranean monk seals (*Monarchus monarchus*). This, and the so-far near-pristine environment, are the reasons why environmentalists are lobbying for protected status (like that for Laganás Bay) for this region.

The hill villages retain much of their traditional architecture and character. Many pre-earthquake buildings survive, though most are too dangerous to live in. One factor that has contributed to their preservation is that no-one can use the damaged buildings unless they have the permission of the owners.

Kerí and Agalás

On the western side of the southern cape – best crossed by the spectacular but rough road from Marathiá – is the pretty village of **Kerí ❺**. Many of the traditional houses here have been bought up by German and British visitors, giving the village quite a different, and more reserved, character from other places on the island. As well as a 17th-century church, Kerí is known for the *píssa tou Keríou*, or natural tar pools, mentioned by both Herodotus and Pliny. Now dried up, they were previously used for caulking boats. A couple of kilometres down the road is the lighthouse at Cape Kerí.

The minor road north from the village runs through a very attractive wooded valley. It leads to the quiet village of **Agalás**, tucked away in the southwestern part of the island. Next to the church in the centre is the small maritime and natural history museum and art gallery, though, with its erratic opening times you may have to ask around for the key. Further south into the village, at the point where the KTEL buses drop off and pick up, you'll find a café and taverna. Signposted off from the village are some Venetian wells and the Damiános cave; both down towards the sea.

From Agalás head northeast to Lithakiá, where you can get acquainted with the olive oil-making process at the **Aristeon Olive Press and Museum ❻** (www.aristeon.gr). It's a modern working factory where you can learn about the methods of olive oil production and how they have changed over time, see the old machinery and get your questions answered by a very well-informed guide. Of course, you can also taste and buy the olive oil in a range of flavours (the bitter orange is surprisingly good),

Venetian ruins

One notable feature of the landscape is the ruined stone towers on the tops of the hills. These are the remains of Venetian windmills, previously used for pumping water up from wells.

Loúha village

together with some delicious local bread.

Kiloméno and Loúha

At the top of the long, steep climb from Maherádo (see page 36) is **Kiloméno ❼**. One place that is definitely worth a visit here is Alitzerinoi, a family-run traditional taverna where you can have a drink or meal. The restaurant is set in an 18th-century stone building with a large outdoor area, arranged into several terraces, all with lovely views of the surrounding villages. Opposite is the somewhat odd-looking church of Ágios Nikólaos, with its unfinished bell tower.

Leaving Kiloméno, the road leads on to the friendly, if a little lacklustre, village of Ágios Léon. Look out for the Venetian windmill converted into a church tower. A road heading inland from here goes up to **Loúha ❽**, one of the highest, and certainly one of the prettiest, settlements on Zákynthos. The domestic architecture of the hill villages differs from that of the rest of the island; plain exteriors hide pretty courtyards, usually full of flowers, with the living quarters set around them. To get a better look at this arrangement pay a visit to Loúha's tiny village shop and post office (opposite the church of Ioánnis Theológos). The courtyard behind, with a 400-year-old floor, has an attractive taverna on the first floor (with the added bonus of excellent toilets). The previously equally attractive village of Gýrio, just beyond Loúha, has been rather spoilt by a breeze-block factory.

The majority of Zákynthos's high mountain villages are controlled by the KKE (Greek communist party). The communists have organised collective agricultural cooperatives to help local farmers buy machinery, and then harvest and market their produce.

From Ágios Léon a pretty but winding, and initially very narrow, road leads down to **Limniónas** by the sea. All that is here is a taverna that looks out over a beautiful rocky bay. Beside the taverna a flight of steps leads down to a small bathing platform.

Éxo Hóra to Anafonítria

The main road carries on north to **Éxo Hóra**. At the crossroads at the village centre is a huge olive tree, reputedly the oldest on the island. The crossroads is also the turn-off for **Kambí**, where a large concrete cross glowers down on the sea from a tall headland. The cross commemorates the place where right-wing soldiers threw a group of local communists to their death in the war, or vice versa, depending whose version of the story you believe.

The unspoilt village of **Mariés** lies further north. Local legend claims Mary Magdalena landed here on her way to or from Rome. This accounts for what seems to be a disproportionate number of churches for the village's size, and for its name (derived from María).

Where the road turns east towards the village of Orthoniés, there is a turn left for **Anafonítria ❾**. Ágios Dionýsios was abbot at the 14th-century monastery here from 1578 to his death in 1622. Further on, above the turn for Navágio, is the 16th-century monastery of **Ágios Geórgios ton Krimnón**, with its striking round tower.

The Blue Caves

Navágio Bay

Just beyond Anafonítria is the headland overlooking **Navágio Bay** (Shipwreck Bay) ❿ – a sheltered bay where a rusty freighter lies half-buried in sand. It is the most photographed beach in the Ionians. The locals take great exception to the disfigurement of their spectacular beach (it was previously known as Paradise Beach) and decry the fact that the boat is now regarded as a tourist icon – it was scuttled by an unscrupulous captain, allegedly a smuggler, for a fraudulent insurance claim.

However, looking down the sheer cliffs from the small steel-viewing platform above is quite spectacular and, for anyone with even a mild distrust of heights, quite stomach churning. Boat trips shuttle sightseers to the beach from **Pórto Vrómi**, below Mariés. The bigger operators are perhaps best avoided for environmental reasons; boats above a certain size are not supposed to land on the beach, but they invariably do.

Back on the main road, heading further north brings you to Volímes.

THE NORTH

North of Alykés the landscape becomes more desolate, rugged and deserted. It was this part of the island that felt the strongest tremors of the 1953 earthquake; the epicentre was in the channel between northern Zákynthos and Kefaloniá.

The long climb out of **Katastári** (the largest village outside the capital) gives views back to Alykés Bay and over to Kefaloniá. After passing the 16th-century Moní Ágios Ioánnis Prodrómou, with an important icon by Theodore Poulakis, you reach the turn-off for Mariés. The road that heads over to the west coast passes through some stunning scenery.

The road along the east coast then plunges down a very steep (10 percent) hill, passing by **Xýngi** ⑪ (see box) and around a headland with numerous sea caves, to the beach at **Makrýs Gialós**. Here, there is a camping ground, several places to eat and sea caves you can swim into right by the beach. About 0.5km (550 yards) further on is the tiny headland of **Kokkínou**, where you can pick up a kaïki (boat) to the Blue Caves and eat overlooking the boats bobbing in the small inlet.

Beyond Kokkínou is the turn-off for the two mountain villages of **Volímes**, famous for their honey and textiles, as well as their surviving traditional mountain architecture.

The road hugs the coast from here to the small port of **Ágios Nikólaos**, where

Odorous beach

The sulphurous smell that wafts around the coast at the tiny bay of Xýngi – surrounded by steep walls of rock – emanates from a hot spring in one of the nearby sea caves.

there are summer ferries to Kefaloniá, but it is best to get boats to the **Blue Caves** ⓬ from the spectacularly located lighthouse at Cape Skinári, the extreme northern tip of the island. The water in the caves appears bright blue, and appears to colour your skin as you swim (see page 38).

KEFALONIÁ

Dramatic, rugged and mountainous, Kefaloniá is the largest and highest Ionian island, rising to 1,627m (5,338ft) at the summit of Mount Énos. Although, or perhaps because, tourism is a relatively recent phenomenon on the island, sparked off in part by the book and film, *Captain Corelli's Mandolin* (see page 69), Kefaloniá has one of the least spoilt environments and some of the best beaches in the Ionian Islands. The south is dominated by the heights of Mount Énos, bordered on the west by the Livathó Plain. In the west is the quiet Pallíki Peninsula, while the stunning north coast is fringed by dramatic cliffs.

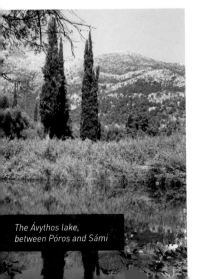
The Ávythos lake, between Póros and Sámi

ARGOSTÓLI

The island's capital, and also its largest town, **Argostóli** ⓭ was completely destroyed in the 1953 earthquake and has been rebuilt largely with modern concrete buildings. Although it is essentially a port and administrative centre, the town is not entirely devoid of charm. It has a great position on the Argostóli Gulf surrounded by mountains, as well as a number of interesting museums, and it makes a good base for exploring the rest of the island. Life in Argostóli centres around Platía Valiánou (the central square) and the pedestrianised shopping street of Lithóstroto.

Seismic emigration

The 1953 earthquake devastated almost all of Kefaloniá – except the far north – causing a huge exodus of refugees. Many settled in Australia, Canada and the US, although recent years have seen families returning to the island.

The Archaeological Museum

On P. Vergóti, close to the theatre and opposite the beginning of Lithóstroto, is Argostóli's **Archaeological Museum Ⓐ** (Tue–Sun 8.30am–3pm; tel 26710 28300). Although small – the museum has just three rooms – the finds are well displayed and help to build up a picture of Kefaloniá's ancient history.

The first room has artefacts from the Palaeolithic to Mycenaean periods and on the left-hand wall are some interesting archive photos (1899–1933) of excavations on the island. The pieces on display range from very early flint hand tools (100,000–40,000 years old), to clay figurines (c.3rd century BC) from the cult centre of the Nymphs at the Drákinas Cave near Póros. The cave had been a settlement from late Neolithic times (8,000 BC onwards). The final case has finds (mostly *kantharos*, or double-handled pots) from the late-middle Helladic cist (box-shaped) graves (1750–1700 BC) and Mycenaean tholos (beehive) tombs at Kokkoláta, southeast of Argostóli.

Ancient trade link

One of the most interesting exhibits in Room 2 of the Archaeological Museum is an Egyptian scarab from the reign of Tuthmosis III (1504–1450 BC). It was found in a Mycenaean site at Kráni, indicating that there was trade between Kefaloniá and pharaonic Egypt.

Room 2 is given over to finds from Mycenaean, or Mycenaean-influenced sites. By now the visitor will have noticed a certain grave and tomb theme to the exhibits. Perhaps the most important finds in this room come from the tholos tomb at Tzannáta near Póros. These include some delicately beaten gold, one piece of which shows the Mycenaean double-axe, clay figurines and an intriguing bronze buckle, indicating the existence of a powerful Mycenaean centre, probably related to Homeric Ithaca. It is thought that this will be vital evidence in pinpointing the exact location of the mythical kingdom.

The third and final room has displays of pieces from the Classical and Roman eras. On the left are a few larger exhibits, including a charming trident and dolphin floor mosaic from the 2nd-century BC sanctuary of Poseidon at Váltsa, on the Pallíki Peninsula. The cases on the right mostly contain pieces from the four ancient cities of Kefaloniá (see page 15). Notable exhibits include an exquisite gold, winged Niké from Menegáta, a marble head of Silenus from Skiniás and a Roman 3rd-century AD bronze male head from Sámi.

The Korgialénios Museum

Up the hill, past the theatre, is the fascinating **Korgialénios Museum and Library** Ⓑ (Ilía Zervoú; Mon 9am–noon, 6–9pm, Tue–Fri 9am–2pm, 6–9pm, Sat 10am–2pm; tel 26710 28835). Set up after the 1953 earthquake to house objects salvaged from the wreckage, the museum gives an overview of 19th-century Kefalonian domestic life. One of the refreshing aspects of the museum is its concentration on the lives and world of Kefalonian women, albeit mostly of the urban middle class. To this end, the displays start with a case of household linen, as well as items such as kid gloves, silk stockings and hair-pins. What follows is an amazing collection of urban women's costume between 1878 and 1910. They are displayed in period interiors, which give an excellent impression of the life of the Kefalonian aristocracy at the end of the 19th century.

For the most part, the dresses are highly elaborate and beautifully made in lace, silk and satin, with appliqué. There is a lovely pair of bridal shoes from 1905 and particularly exquisite is a young girl's ball gown of 1894, with silk tulle and

Ancient pottery on display at the Archaeological Museum

embroidered roses. There are also a great number of accessories, including shawls, fans, parasols and gloves.

The museum also has a good display of photographs of pre-1953 Argostóli. The earliest, from 1904–6 and taken by local photographer N. Trikardos, show it as a neat, provincial town. Some of the later (1930s) pictures were taken by two members of the Kosmetatou family. More disturbing are the images showing the total devastation of the town after the 1953 earthquake.

Other displays include a room with some rather dark and heavy furniture and portraits of local worthies, a lovely 18th-century carved and painted wooden iconostasis from the church of Agíou Georgíou, and a case with the effects of Dimitrios Korgialenios (died 1861), a member of the secret pro-independence Filikí Etería (Society of Friends). Finally, after a cluttered but cosy reconstruction of a traditional bedroom, there are displays of agricultural implements.

The Foká-Kosmetátou Foundation

Back towards the central *platía*, at the far end of Valliánou, is a beautifully restored neoclassical mansion housing the **Foká-Kosmetátou Foundation** ❻ (www.focas-cosmetatos.gr; May–Oct Mon–Fri 10am–2pm). The foundation, which was established in 1984 from the estates of three brothers, turned their family home into a museum to display their private collections and to publish studies on Kefaloniá; it has also established the Votanókypos Kefaloniás on

> #### No-nonsense praise
>
> 'The buildings of Argostóli are handsome, and the town, though not remarkable for its liveliness, possesses many good streets and public edifices.'
> Edward Lear, *Views in the Seven Ionian Islands*, 1863

the outskirts of town (see page 58).

Strolling down Lithóstroto, Argostóli

The museum consists of just one room with, on the right, a display of Greek numismatics and, opposite, a number of lithographs of the Ionians and some pieces of furniture that belonged to the family. Of greatest interest are the lithographs by Joseph Cartwright, Edward Lear and Henry Cook, all of whom published volumes of paintings and engravings of the Ionians. Close by is a fine icon of Ágios Vikédios attributed to Theodoros Poulakis. Also look out for the 10 drachma bank note from the 1890s, cut in half; each half then became worth five drachmas. The small but pretty garden at the back is used to hold temporary exhibitions.

Lithóstroto and the Drápano Bridge

The main shopping street of Argostóli is the pedestrianised **Lithóstroto**, which runs south from P. Vergóti, the site of the town's theatre. Reconstructed after the 1953 earthquake, during the 19th and early-20th century the theatre, with its largely Italian opera productions, was the centre of the social life of Argostóli's middle class. Lithóstroto is lined with cafés, rivals to those in the central *platía*, and pricey clothing and shoe shops. About halfway down, on the right-hand side, is the town's Catholic church. Heavily restored following the

Drápano Bridge

earthquake, its chief claim to fame is the 14th-century icon of the Panagía Prevezána. Beyond the church is the **Pýrgos Kabánas** (Kabána Tower). This reconstructed late 18th-century Venetian bell tower now houses a pleasant café decorated with pre-earthquake photographs of Argostóli.

At the end of the pedestrianised section of Lithóstroto, turn left down towards the harbour. On the left is the town's produce market. Depending on the season it is piled high with all kinds of colourful agricultural produce.

Walking south along the water brings you to the **Drápano Bridge**. This stone-built causeway crosses the shallow Koútavos Lagoon but is closed due to structural damage. Built by the British in 1810, it was overseen by Major de Bosset, Commandant of Kefaloniá, a Swiss soldier in the service of the British army. The obelisk in the centre has an inscription to the supposed glories of the British Empire.

The Katavóthres

Rizospáston heads north from the central *platía*. On your right you will pass Argostóli's **Filarmonikí Skholí** (Philharmonic School), and opposite, on the corner of the next block, the only building to have survived the 1953 earthquake intact. The streets running off to the right will take you down to the harbour.

By the port authority buildings (near where the ferries depart) is Argostóli's helpful **EOT** (tourist information office). Further along, past the place on the quay where you catch the ferry for Lixoúri, is a line of *estiatória* (restaurants), the best of which is Kyani Akti (see page 108). Before that, on the left, is a small square. On a small patch of grass is the marble base of a Venetian fountain, with carved lions' heads. The column above it is of later (19th-century) provenance.

Continue along the coast, past a couple of very pleasant tavernas and down a pine-shaded footpath beside the rocks, where local people swim in the evening. After about a kilometre (0.6 miles), you reach the tip of the cape. The views here over the mountains and the Argostóli Gulf are spectacular. Also here are the *Katavóthres* ⑭, or sea mills, which are the product of a bizarre geological phenomenon. Seawater from the gulf disappears down a series of small sink-holes, only to re-emerge in the cave of Melissáni and under the Gulf of Sámi on the opposite side of the island. The water passes through channels cut by subterranean fresh-water streams during the last ice

Column of light

On a short promontory at Cape Ágios Theódoros is a Doric-colonnaded light-house dating from 1820. It was commissioned by Charles Napier, who was the British Governor of Kefaloniá between 1822 and 1830.

The katavóthres (sea mills) near Argostóli

age, when seawater levels were lower. Fresh water filtering down through the limestone hills increases the flow. As the channels widen the now-brackish water slows, before its resurgence.

The current at the Argostóli end was strong enough in the past to drive mills, built by the British to grind grain. After the 1953 earthquake the flow was disrupted and slowed to the gently running channels you see today. The original mills were destroyed in 1953 and replaced by a fake water wheel and a café, very popular with locals for Sunday lunch. Further on, around the cape, are a series of small bays where you can swim.

Votanókypos Kefaloniás

Leaving town to the south, following Leofóros Georgíou Vergóti, brings you to a fork in the road. The left carries on to Peratáta, the right-hand turn has a signpost to the **Votanókypos Kefaloniás** ⑮ (Cephalonia Botanica; www.focas-cosmetatos. gr; May–Oct Mon–Sat 9am–2.30pm). Follow the signs and don't be put off by the rough track, as it soon levels out. Bear left at the top of the rise and the site is 50m (160ft) along on your right. Entrance is free with a ticket to the Foká-Kosmetátou Foundation (see page 54), otherwise leave your money in the honesty box in the hut at the entrance.

This botanical garden was established in 2000 in an old olive grove. Its aim is to represent the rich flora of the different environments found on Kefaloniá, as well as seeking to preserve rare and endangered Kefalonian plants. The garden is allied to the Millennium Seed Bank at London's Kew Gardens. The site is beautiful and a world away from the nearby warehouses on the main road. An artificial stream runs through the centre of well laid-out and labelled areas, while in spring and early summer it is lovely to see the floor of the remaining olive grove carpeted with flowers, rather than the ploughed-up versions usually seen from the roadside.

THE LIVATHÓ AND SOUTH COAST

To the south of Argostóli is the **Livathó Plain**, one of the few level areas on the island. Not surprisingly it is largely given over to agriculture. The road out of town bisects the plain, passing the castle of Agíou Georgíou above the villages of Peratáta and Mazarakáta (site of a Mycenaean necropolis), before, dominated by the bulk of Mount Énos to the east, it hugs the southern coast along to the resort of Skála.

The gardens at Votanókypos Kefaloniás

Kástro Agíou Georgíou

Towering above the plain is the **Kástro Agíou Georgíou** ⑯ (mid-June–Oct

Tue–Sun 8.30am–3pm), constantly being renovated and liable to closure. The fortress stands on a pine-clad hill, and can be reached from the north by the turn-off for the Robola Wine Cooperative or via the hairpinned road from Peratáta. Either route brings you up to the Bórgo, the village outside the castle's walls. The view from the top is spectacular, and the Castle or Kastro Café is a good place to take it in, particularly if you have just walked up in the heat and are in need of refreshment.

There has been a fortress on the site since Byzantine times, centred around the church of Agíou Georgíou from which the castle takes its name. In 1185 the island was taken by the Franks, and the fort was controlled by them until 1485. After a brief period of Turkish rule, the castle passed to the Venetians in 1500 following a three-month siege.

Kástro Agíou Georgíou

The fortifications seen today largely date from the period of Venetian occupation. At this time the castle was the centre of the island's administration, but in 1757 the Venetians moved their official headquarters down to Argostóli, heralding the fort's decline. Like all buildings in southern Kefaloniá, the castle suffered great damage in the 1953 earthquake. However, it is well worth a visit for the view and renovated walls.

Back down in Peratáta, just beyond the village, is the turn for **Moní Agíou Andréou** (also confusingly known as **Moní Milapidiás**). The convent is now housed in modern (post-1953) buildings. Opposite these is the old church of Ágios Andréas, home to important 16th- to 18th-century icons by, among others, Immanuel Lambardos and Athanassios Anninos (1713–48). These are now

Icon from Moní Agíou Andréou

part of the **Ecclesiastical Museum** (www.new.imk.gr; daily 7am–2pm, 5pm–9pm). As well as good Ionian School paintings, the well-laid-out museum has reliquaries allegedly containing remains of Ágios Andréas and some ecclesiastical vestments.

Lássi and Metaxáta

A low but steep range of hills separates the Livathó Plain and Argostóli from the west coast. This hides some pretty villages, a couple of good wineries and, on the western side, attractive beaches. From Argostóli take either the main road out towards Lakíthra (then follow the signposts to the airport), or go around the cape via Ágios Theódoros and a number of bays, along a pleasant pine-flanked road. Both routes are walkable and will bring you to Lássi, the closest resort to Argostóli.

By Greek island standards **Lássi** is fairly low-key, although it does get crowded in high season. The star beaches here are **Makrýs** and **Platýs Gialós**, both with fine sand and clean, blue water. The latter has a small island attached to the beach by a short isthmus. The coastal road continues south above cliffs with lovely views. After a couple of kilometres (1.2 miles) is the **Gentilini Winery** (www.gentilini.gr; tours and tastings May–June daily 11am–8pm, July–Sept daily 11am–8.30pm, Oct Mon–Sat 11am–6.30pm). Owned by the Kosmetatou family, the winery was established in 1984 and specialises in high-quality organic wines, including a fine Robola.

Above Miniá, close to the airport, is the pretty village of Sarláta, topped by a rather Gothic, ivy-clad ruin. There are a number of rooms and villas to let here. Just along from Sarláta

The beach at Lássi

is **Domáta**, with an impressive church and houses spilling down the hillside. The church of the Panagía here contains the coffin in which the remains of Patriarch Grigoris V were transported from Istanbul to Odessa. It also has an interesting 19th-century wooden iconostasis.

The next village is **Metaxáta**, chiefly famous as the place where Byron stayed for four months in 1823 before leaving for Mesolóngi on the mainland, where he died. A bust of the poet can be seen in the main square, close to the site of the house where he stayed (destroyed in 1953). Below Metaxáta and Domáta is **Kourkoumeláta**, close to the lovely beach of Ávythos. The attractive village was rebuilt by Andreas Vergotis after 1953. At **Pesáda**, where seasonal ferries leave for Ágios Nikólaos on Zákynthos, is the **Divino Winery** (summer daily 10am–8pm) which produces a traditional Muscat, made from sun-dried grapes.

Lourdáta to Skála

From the long beach at **Lourdáta**, just past Pesáda, to the village of Markópoulo there is little apart from **Moní Theotókou Sisíon**, believed to have been founded by St Francis of Assisi. The road south from here is fairly bleak, though towards the coast the land appears more fertile. After the right turn-off to Skála, the road rises towards **Markópoulo** ⓱. The church of the Panagía here is the scene of a bizarre festival. Between the 6th and 15th of August hundreds of small, harmless snakes appear, said to bring good luck to the village.

Taking the left-hand turn to Skála takes you first past **Kateliós**, and then the long sweep of sand of **Kamínia**. Before reaching Kateliós you might want to call in at the **Metaxas Wine Estate** (May–Oct Mon–Fri 10.30am–2.30pm) and taste their excellent Robola. Kateliós is a tiny, laid-back resort with a lovely sandy beach, on the opposite side of the bay from Kamínia. This

Pebbled shoreline between Póros and Skála

is Kefaloniá's most important nesting beach for loggerhead turtles, although fewer nest here than on Zákynthos. Visitors should treat this area with respect and follow the national park guidelines (see page 40). In truth it shouldn't be necessary to disturb the turtles as just along the coast is **Skála**, a popular, but relatively tasteful resort on a huge sandy beach backed by pine-clad hills. Also here, a little inland, are the excavated remains of a Roman villa with some fine, preserved mosaics.

MOUNT ÉNOS

The highest mountain in the Ionian islands is **Mount Énos ⑱**. At 1,627m (5,338ft) it dominates the southern part of Kefaloniá. Also known by its Venetian name of Monte Nero (the black mountain), its upper reaches are covered by the Greek fir (*Abies cephalonica*), giving the mountain a dark cap. The fir was first identified on the island (hence its Latin name) and the Énos population is particularly important due to its lack of hybridisation. It is generally found at altitudes of between 800 and 1,600m (2,600–5,250ft) and grows up to 30m (100ft) high. It was an important tree to the ancient Greeks, who used it extensively in shipbuilding.

Énos National Park

The indigenous population of firs is now protected by the **Énos National Park**. This takes in the summit of Mount Énos above 1,000m (3,280ft) and the northern flanks of neighbouring Mount Roúdi (also called Gioúpari; 1,124m/3,687ft). The two mountains are divided by a high saddle, which is marred by a NATO radar station bristling with satellite dishes. A new tarmac road runs up to the saddle from the main road between Argostóli and Sámi. From the telecom masts it's another 1km (0.6 miles) downhill on an unpaved road to a slightly wider stretch where you can park (be warned it is rough going, and don't be tempted to drive any further than this point). A signposted footpath ascends to the summit, Megas Soros. If it is not too hazy the views from the top are incomparable.

The turn-off towards Valsamáta will take you to the **Cephalonian Robola Producers Cooperative** at Frangáta (www.robola.gr; summer daily 9am–8pm, winter daily 9am–3pm). The Robola grape is cultivated on the high altitude limestone soils found in the region and is used to

Feral ponies

The semi-wild ponies of Mount Énos are descended from animals abandoned after World War II. They initially formed communities of up to 100 animals but are now highly endangered, numbering only some 12–14 individuals. If you are lucky enough to spot them, be careful not to disturb them.

produce a fine white wine. The cooperative makes two Robola wines, both of which can be tasted in the visitors' centre.

Close to the winery, just beyond Valsamáta, is **Moní Agíou Gerasímou** (daily 9am–1pm and 4–8pm). Ágios Gerasímos is the patron saint of Kefaloniá, and the convent, founded in the 16th century, is the most important pilgrimage site on the island. The (male) saint founded a female order in 1554 and was beatified in 1622.

Inside the new convent church, consecrated in 1992, is the saint's silver shrine, inside which is the reliquary containing his bones; his funeral robes are draped over the shrine. Although the church is new, it still contains many fine original works of art, as well as a staircase that descends to a couple of small chambers, thought to be the saint's sanctuary.

SÁMI AND PÓROS

The road from Argostóli over the flanks of Mount Énos descends past fir-clad slopes to the small port of **Sámi**. Ferries leave from here for the island of Itháki and Pátra, on the mainland. Sámi is a pleasant, quiet town with a few eating places along the harbourfront. This town was the location for much of the filming of *Captain Corelli's Mandolin* in 2000 (see page 69). For the filming, much of Sámi's

Goat on the flanks of Mount Énos

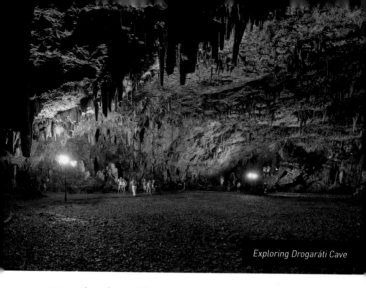
Exploring Drogaráti Cave

pre-earthquake architecture was reconstructed, only to be destroyed during the subsequent battle scenes.

Over the headland of Cape Dihália (also known as Mýtikas) is the beautiful white shingle beach of **Andísamos ⑳**, also used as a location for the film. Surrounded by steep, maquis-clad hills, the deep inlet looks out on the southern coast of Itháki. The clear water is great for swimming; the furthest little bay of the beach is nudist.

The Drogaráti and Melissáni Caves

On the road from Argostóli, about 3km (2 miles) before Sámi, is the turn for the **Drogaráti Cave ㉑** (Apr–Oct daily 9am–8pm). The cave was discovered about 300 years ago, after an earthquake opened up the present entrance. A steep series of steps leads down into a cool fissure, at the bottom of which is a concrete viewing platform overlooking the huge chamber. Occasionally

Looking out over Póros

used to hold concerts, it has an impressive array of stalactites. Some of these are damaged, broken off by unthinking souvenir hunters, but there is still a huge amount of flowstone left. From the platform you can make your way down on to the floor of the chamber, where you can explore the nooks and crannies. To see the chamber at its best, wait until the tour groups have departed, when you can explore on your own.

Perhaps even more impressive is the cave lake at **Melissáni** ㉒ (May–Oct daily 8am–7pm, Nov–Apr Thu, Sat, Sun 10am–4pm), west of Sámi. A short artificial tunnel brings you to the edge of a large underground lake, partly open to the sky due to the collapse of the cavern's roof; the sunlight on the deep, clear water turns it an iridescent blue. Visitors are rowed around the lake by waiting boatmen.

The cave was formed between 20,000 and 16,000 years ago, during the last ice age. The roof of the cavern collapsed some 5,000 years ago, the debris from which still lies in the centre of the lake. Perhaps the most fascinating aspect of its geology is that it is the point of resurgence for the water that sinks at the katavóthres near Argostóli, hence the water in the cave is brackish. It enters the lake at its deepest point (32m/104ft) on the left-hand side, and sinks again at the far point of the covered section of the cave which lies to your right.

It was in the still intact section of the cavern that archaeological finds were made, dating from the 4th–3rd century BC, confirming that the cave had been the site of a cult of Pan and the Nymphs.

⊙ CAPTAIN CORELLI'S MANDOLIN

This novel, by the British author Louis de Bernières and set in Kefaloniá during World War II, was first published in 1994 and became a bestseller through word of mouth. The book concerns the exploits of Antonio Corelli, a mandolin-playing captain in the occupying Italian army, and Pelagia, daughter of the local doctor. The core of the text is a love story but this is also set against the German invasion of 1943, after the capitulation of the Italians, and the subsequent massacre of Italian troops, and any islander found helping them, by the German army. Add in the Greek communist resistance, a ridiculous upper-class English intelligence officer who can only speak ancient Greek and a film tie-in starring Nicolas Cage and Penélope Cruz, shot on location on Kefaloniá, and you have the Captain Corelli phenomenon.

Although the book has been an international success with the reading public (despite being famously slow to get into), it has stirred up the passions of locals and historians alike. Their major objection is the book's portrayal of the communist resistance (known by the acronym ELAS). Well-loved and regarded as national heroes by many Greeks – and aided in this case by Italian fighters – its portrayal in the book is suspect. The strong anti-communist – and historically inaccurate – bias to the text defames not only the movement as a whole, but, more specifically, a surviving partisan, Amos Pampaloni, on whose life it seems to have been based, and who objected strongly to this historical mistreatment.

From the cave, near Karavómylos, the coast road runs north around the bay of Sámi, to the small port of **Agía Efimía Ierous**. This attractive yachting harbour has a great location, with steep, bare mountainsides looming behind and a sweeping view over the bay to Itháki. The town's narrow shingle beach, north of the yachting harbour – now backed by rather brutal concrete sea walls – has wonderfully clear water and the swimming here is excellent.

Póros

The main road south from Sámi passes through some beautiful countryside, as well as the attractive mountain villages of Digaléto and Ágios Nikólaos, which are close to the **Ávythos Lake**. Just beyond Ágios Nikólaos, on the hairpin bends, are the ruins of a monastery. From here the road runs straight down to the village of Tzanáta.

Tzanáta lies in a fertile bowl. On a small rise in the vale is a Mycenaean tholos (beehive) tomb, excavated in 1992–4. The earliest finds date from c.1350 BC and the high quality of the artefacts – including jewellery, pottery and seals – points to the existence of a powerful Mycenaean centre. It is thought that this may identify Tzanáta as the location of Homeric Ithaca.

Between Tzanáta and Póros the road passes through the short but impressive 80-m (260-ft) deep **Póros Gorge 23**, the channel for a seasonal river. The town of **Póros** is divided by a rocky headland, on the far side of which is the port and fishing harbour. Ferries sail from here to Kyllíni on the mainland. The Remetzo café/bar at the foot of the jetty is pleasant and also has surprisingly good toilets. As a resort, Póros has a quiet, pleasantly run-down air. The 2-km (1.2-mile) long pebbly town beach has very clear water and there are some secluded rocky bays around the headland.

To the north of town is the long beach of Rágia, above which is **Moní Theotókou Átrou** (take the right turn just after the gorge on leaving town). This is said to be the oldest monastery on Kefaloniá, first mentioned in 1264. The beautiful road south to Skála runs along the deserted coastline. Before reaching Skála, at Ágios Geórgios, there are the (minimal) remains of a classical temple to Apollo.

THE PALLÍKI PENINSULA

On the opposite (western) side of the gulf from Argostóli is the large Pallíki Peninsula (also known as the Lixoúri Peninsula), which, away from its south coast, is barely touched by tourism. On the southeast coast is its major town, Argostóli's traditional rival Lixoúri.

Lixoúri

Easily reached by an hourly ferry (around 20 minutes), **Lixoúri** now plays second fiddle to Argostóli and is a sleepy, laid-back place. However, it's worth taking the ferry for the views of the gulf alone and there are a number of sights worth seeing in the town. It is also a good jumping off point for other places on the peninsula.

Lixoúri developed under Venetian rule (becoming officially recognised in 1534), but about 1.5km (1 mile) north of town is

Xí beach

the site of ancient Pali, one of the four ancient city states of the island (see page 15). Much of Lixoúri was destroyed in 1953 but a few major buildings have been reconstructed as before. The earliest of these is the collonaded Markáto, just behind the seafront where the Argostóli ferry docks. It was built in 1824 by the British governor, Charles Napier, and was Kefaloniá's first courtroom. Many of Lixoúri buildings suffered damage to some extent in the 2014 earthquake.

Further along, on Grígoris Labráki, is the **Filarmonikí Skholí Pállis** (Philharmonic School), in a fine neoclassical building dated 1836 (rebuilt in 1963). There are four such 'schools' – wind and brass ensembles, a legacy of British rule – on the island: here, in Argostóli, and in Sámi and Póros. Wind instruments including the flute of founder, Petros Skarlatos (1820–1904), are on show in the prettily decorated first-floor rehearsal room.

Also in the town, up the hill on Ekaterínis (from the port walk up Pávlou Dellapórta, then Mihaïl Avílhou) is the **Lixoúri Museum and Library** (closed following the 2015 earthquake). Set in an attractive 1866 neoclassical building with a shady garden, the library holds around 25,000 volumes. The attached museum has three early gospels, as well as 18th- and 19th-century ecclesiastical vestments.

On the waterfront is a statue of local satirical writer and poet Andreas Laskaratos (1811–1901), his back turned on Argostóli across the water. The early nationalist writer Elias Miniates (1669–1714) was also born here.

The south and east coasts

To the south is the plain of Katogís, the most fertile area on the island, planted with wheat and vines. This suffered greatly in the 1953 earthquake and the effect on the now-fractured topography is obvious. The southern coast has some lovely beaches, and the most popular and spectacular are the red sand stretches of **Mégas Lákkos** and its continuation, **Xí ㉔**.

North of Xí is the village of Madzavináta, unremarkable except for the **Vitoratos Winery** (summer daily 10am–2pm and 6–8pm). Beyond Madzaninata is **Havriáta**. As well as the church of **Iperagías Theotókou**, it is the location of the school of Vikentiou Damodou (1700–52), one of the first on the island. Back towards Lixoúri is **Soullári**, with its church of

No more rocking

Just along from Xí beach, close to Cape Akrotíri, is the Kounópetra (the name literally means, 'rocking stone'). This flat slab of stone used to rock in the waves, but the 1953 earthquake disturbed its balance, so that it no longer moves.

View of Ássos

Agías Marínas, dating from 1600 and containing icons by the Cretan painters Immanuel Moskos and Theodoros Poulakis. The water dripping down in the cave at Moní Agías Paraskevís, by the beach at **Lépeda**, allegedly cures eye infections.

North of town, past the port of ancient Pali at Karavostási, is the monastery of the Panagías at **Kehriónos**; a festival is held here on 23 August. Some 5km (3 miles) further on is a small but important wetland area near the village of **Livádi**.

Anogí

The northern and western mountainous part of the peninsula is known as Anogí. At the southern end of the wild and deserted west coast is the monastery of **Theotókou Kipouríon**, founded in 1759. Perched high on the cliffs, this can be a spectacular place to watch the sunset. Below is the sea cave of **Drakospilía** (dragon's cave). There is a spring at the nearby ruined church of Agía Paraskeví that is said to cure stomach ailments. Some 10km (6 miles) up the coast – longer by the winding roads – is undoubtedly the finest beach on the peninsula, **Petaní** ㉕, a beautiful stretch of pebbles backed by steep cliffs.

Before reaching Petaní you pass through the village of **Kodogenáda**. In addition to its restored 18th- and 19th-century vernacular architecture, the village is home to two important churches, the 12th- to 13th-century Agíou Georgíou and Agíou Ioánni tou Theológou, with its impressive carved iconostasis.

THE NORTH

The north of Kefaloniá escaped the worst of the ravages of the 1953 earthquake and so has much surviving traditional architecture. The landscape is barren and spectacularly steep, particularly along the **west coast road**, which is the best, if most alarming, ride on the island.

Northwest coast villages

From Argostóli the road takes you past the turning for the village of **Davgáta**, the location of the **Museum of Natural History** (summer Mon–Fri 9am–1.30pm, Sat–Sun 9am–1pm; winter Sun–Fri 9am–1.30pm). Set up as an educational centre and library, it provides a useful introduction to the local geology, flora and fauna.

The coast road continues to Fársa, where it starts to climb. Above is the old village, ruined in 1953. Below, and along this whole stretch of coast, you can see rows of fish farms. Beyond Angónas

Picturesque prison

Dating from the late 16th century, the fortress at Ássos was used as a prison until 1953. The prisoners tended the vines that covered the hillsides and clifftops above Ássos village.

the view along the northwest coast opens up – a steep line of cliffs falling into blue sea. Down to the west are the beaches of **Agía Kyriakí** and **Voúti**. The long, exposed stretch of sand at Agía Kyriakí can attract flotsam but the small bay at Voúti, down a rough unmade road from the village of Zóla, is cleaner. Although the water isn't the island's clearest, it can get very warm here, even in early summer.

From here onward the sharp hairpins of the road hug the cliff edges. This is Kefaloniá's equivalent of the oceanside Highway 1 in California. The views – back to the largely inaccessible north coast of Pallíki and forward to Ássos – are wonderful.

Mýrtos and Ássos

Some 10km (6 miles) beyond Angónas the road turns sharply inland, forming a large hairpin around the truly spectacular bay of **Mýrtos** ㉖. The best place to see the beach and cliffs is from the lay-by on the main road on the northern side of the bay. Looking down, you see a crescent of bright white beach bordered by the cornflower blue of the sea and surrounded by sheer cliffs. The way down to the beach is via the steep but well-paved road from Divaráta. Once there, it does not quite live up to its view from above. What appeared to be white sand turns out to be small pebbles, and it can get very busy. The beach also feels too organised, with sunbeds, a café and life-guards – essential, as the sea can be dangerous here.

From Divaráta the road continues east (turn left before the village to go north). The road crosses the island, through a gap in the mountains, to Agía Efimía (see page 49), passing on the way a couple of now derelict Venetian windmills that were previously used for pumping water up from wells.

The road north carries on in a similarly spectacular fashion. About 3km (2 miles) after a viewpoint lay-by is the steep

The bay of Mýrtos

descent to **Ássos** ❷. At the bottom is Ássos village, with its charming natural harbour. The village retains much of its traditional architecture (reconstructed with the help of the City of Paris, commemorated by a plaque in Platía Parísion), and in spring and early summer is covered in flowers. The small beach in the harbour is fairly clean but just round the coast are some beautiful coves, only accessible by boat.

Connected to the village by a short isthmus is an enormous Venetian *kástro* (fort) on top of a hill. Begun in 1593, it served to protect the Venetian fleet and island from attack by the Ottomans and pirates. In more recent history it was used as a prison (see box page 75). The winding path takes you up through pine woods and gives fine views over the harbour and neighbouring coast. Apart from the walls and the lovely curving entrance, little remains inside the fort, although a new visitors' centre has been sensitively built in the middle.

Fiskárdo harbour

Around Fiskárdo

The road beyond Ássos ends up at the harbour of Fiskárdo at the north-eastern tip of the island. This is perhaps the most immediately attractive part of the island, with much surviving traditional vernacular architecture. Two of the most attractive **hill villages** here are **Vasilikiádes**, on the main road 10km (6 miles) before Fiskárdo, and **Mesovoúnia**. The latter is on the eastern road to Agía Efimía. This passes through a string of very pretty mountain villages – **Varý**, **Karyá** and **Komitáta** – and the views over to the neighbouring island of Itháki are magnificent. The only sounds across this landscape, with its dry stone walls and abandoned stone houses, are the tinkling of cow and sheep bells. Water is at a premium here, and there are a number of rainwater cisterns with concrete covered catchments above. The view down to Agía Efimía from Komitáta is breathtaking.

Towards Fiskárdo itself you pass through **Mánganos**, with its excellent greengrocer, full of wonderful local fruit and vegetables, and olives, oil and wine, and **Andipáta Erísou**, the turn-off for Dafnoúdi beach (see page 80). **Fiskárdo** ㉘ itself survived the 1953 earthquake intact, and has cashed in on this with a vengeance. The admittedly very attractive harbourfront is backed by pastel-shaded housing, now largely expensive restaurants, cafés and boutiques.

The harbour, for better or worse, is also greatly beloved by yachters, particularly those on flotilla holidays (it's fun to sit on the quayside watching novice sailors try to bring their boats in for mooring).

The port takes its name from Robert Guiscard, a Norman soldier who died here in 1085, but is thought to be the location of ancient Panormas. There is also a Roman cemetery (2nd–4th centuries AD). Towards the Venetian lighthouse, on the northern headland, is an interesting church, started by the Byzantines, but largely Norman in execution (c.12th century). At the southern end of the harbour is the **Nautical and Environmental Museum** (summer Mon–Sat 10am–6pm, Sun 10am–2pm; donations encouraged). Run by volunteers from the FNEC European exchange programme, it consists of one

Shopping lane in Fiskárdo

Vathý harbour

room with some interesting exhibits, including the skeleton of a Cuvier's beaked whale, found dead on Émblisi beach in 1995, and displays describing local birds and mammals and their habitats.

The northern coast has some wonderful small and quiet **beaches**, all of which have the clearest imaginable water. Some of the little bays, with their white pebble beaches, are only accessible by boat (easily hired for the day in Fiskárdo from Regina's boats, www.fiscardoboatrental.com). The two most easily accessible from Fiskárdo are, to the north, **Émblisi** and, to the south, the beautiful bay of **Fóki**. Heavenly **Dafnoúdi** is reached by a 20-minute walk down through pine trees from the village of Andipáta Erísou. Tiny **Alatiés**, to the south of Dafnoúdi, could be lovely, but attracts tar (and an unfortunate smell), but nearby **Agía Ierousalím** ㉙ is a lot cleaner and has one of the friendliest tavernas on the island, Odisseas (see page 110).

ITHÁKI

Easily visited from Kefaloniá, the island of Itháki has a history that's intimately tied up with that of its larger neighbour. Claimed by many, particularly the locals, to be the mythical homeland of the Homeric hero Odysseus, there is little archaeological evidence to support this claim (indeed, it seems as though Homeric Ithaca is likely to lie close to present-day Póros on Kefaloniá, see page 70). Daily ferries leave from Sámi on Kefaloniá and dock at the tiny harbour of Píso Aetós on the west coast of Itháki.

Like Kefaloniá, Itháki suffered greatly from the 1953 earthquake, causing many people to emigrate (the population dropped from around 15,000 to under 3,000). However, it is a supremely beautiful and unspoilt island with a lovely main town, Vathý, and some gorgeous deserted beaches.

VATHÝ AND THE NORTH

Vathý ⑩ lies on the island's east coast, at the head of a deep bay on the Gulf of Mólou. It is a quiet, very attractive town (it still retains surviving pre-earthquake architecture) with a huge number of tavernas set around its harbourfront and an **Archaeological Museum** (tel 26740 32200; Tue–Sun 8.30am–3.30pm). Ferries depart for Pátra on the mainland.

To the north, the road crosses the isthmus and either heads up to the mountain-top village of Anogí or around the western coast through Léfki. **Anogí**, only occupied for half the year, has fabulous views as well as the Byzantine church of Kímisis tis Theotókou. Before reaching Léfki you pass a series of small, quiet pebble beaches: Vrýsi, Áspros Gialós, Komninoú Ámmos and Koutoúpi.

The roads from both Léfki and Anogí join at

Twin peaks

Itháki is essentially two groups of mountains linked by a narrow isthmus. On the eastern side of the isthmus is the deep Gulf of Mólou, while on the north coast is the large bay of Afáles.

Itháki's main town, Vathý

Stavrós, the island's second-largest town. This sits above the small port of Pólis (a 20-minute walk). There is a small **Archaeological Museum** (Tue–Sun 8.30am–3pm) here, housing local finds. These mostly come from the early Bronze Age to Mycenaean site at nearby Pelikáta, one of the many sites claimed as the location of the palace of Odysseus.

North of Stavrós a road winds up to the hill village of Exogí. On the way up is an excavation known as the School of Homer, in reality a tower dating from the 6th century BC; close by is a Mycenaean tomb. Below is the spectacular bay of **Afáles** ❸❶ with its lovely beach. From the beach at Afáles a rough, but beautiful minor road heads north towards Cape Drákou Pídimia, before doubling back down to the deserted beach at Mármaka.

After the quiet port of Fríkes on the east coast, a favourite yachting harbour, the main road heads around to **Kióni** ❸❷, an attractive place and Itháki's most upmarket resort. Like Fiskárdo on Kefaloniá, Kióni survived the 1953 earthquake, and has capitalised on this in a similar fashion, as evidenced in the prices for accommodation. The coast between Fríkes and Kióni has a number of lovely pebbly beaches. The walk up to Anogí from Kióni, along a clearly marked path, is delightful and takes around 1.5 hours each way.

THE ODYSSEUS TRAIL

The south of the island has a number of sites that are supposedly linked with events in Homer's *The Odyssey* (see page 17). Close to Vathý, up the hill from the beach at Dexá (identified as ancient Phorcys, the landing place of Odysseus), is the **Cave of the Nymphs** ③. This spot is apparently where the Greek hero, helped by the goddess Athene, hid the cauldrons, tripods, cloaks and cups given to him by the Phaeacian king, Alcinous.

Odysseus, transformed by the goddess into an old man, met up with Eumaeus (his old palace swineherd) at the **Arethoúsa Spring** ③, where the pigs were being watered. The spring is in the south of the island, 3km (2 miles) from Vathý, along a steep but well-marked path. Above the spring is the Cave of Eumaeus.

On the other side of the island, towards the harbour and pebble beach at **Píso Aetós**, is the site of **Alalkomenes** (c.700 BC). This was wrongly identified by the German archaeologist Heinrich Schliemann in 1878 as the palace of Odysseus, where the hero came to win back his wife, Penelope, from her suitors.

Above Píso Aetós is the village of **Perahóri**, which is close to the island's now deserted and ruined medieval capital, Paleóhora.

Idyllic Afáles Bay

Swimming at Navágio Beach

WHAT TO DO

SPORTS

The wonderfully clear sea and spectacular mountains of Zákynthos and Kefaloniá invite visitors to do more than just sit in a deck chair looking out at the view. Options for active holidays are numerous, from swimming, diving and sailing to walking, cycling and horse riding.

WATER SPORTS

Swimming. The water quality around the islands is excellent. The water is extremely clear and clean and, in general, safe; though be careful at some of the west-facing beaches, particularly Mýrtos on Kefaloniá, as there can be some very nasty undercurrents. For little children, the southern and eastern beaches of Zákynthos (for example Kalamáki, Pórto Koúkla and Tsiliví) are best, as they have gently sloping sand and calm waters. Otherwise, most hotels and many apartments have swimming pools, though in summer it would be a shame not to take advantage of the warm waters surrounding the islands. At some points (notably the pebbly beaches around the north and eastern coasts of Kefaloniá) the view from the water over to Itháki or Lefkáda is stunning.

Snorkelling and diving. The coasts around Zákynthos and Kefaloniá are a divers' paradise – the rocky shoreline is home to wide variety of creatures, and the calm, clear water gives visibility up to 50m (165ft). All scuba-diving schools have qualified instructors who will choose dive locations according to your experience. Extended boat trips are available for advanced divers. For the more advanced trips, or to hire equipment and go by yourself, you will need to

> **Boat hire**
>
> Hiring a small (25 horse-power) motorboat is the best way to explore secluded and otherwise inaccessible bays. They are available from travel agents in many places (particularly on Kefaloniá) and cost €50–100 per day plus petrol. They are great for swimming from – simply anchor, then dive or jump off the side; all boats have a fold-down ladder to help you get back on board.

show a diving certificate. Most major resorts have reputable diving schools. Well-reputed dive centres approved by the Professional Association of Diving Instructors (PADI; www.padi.com) include Diving Center Turtle Beach at Límni Kerioú (tel: 26950 49424; www.diving-center-turtle-beach.com), on Zákynthos, and Aquatic World in Agía Efimía (tel: 26740 62006; www.aquatic.gr), on Kefaloniá. If you don't want to indulge in full-scale scuba diving, snorkelling with simply a mask, snorkel and flippers can be equally rewarding.

Water sports. Zákynthos is the best island to visit for organised water sports, with major centres located at Tsiliví, Alykés and Ágios Nikólaos on the Vasilikós Peninsula. Boards and sails for windsurfing are available for hire at certain beaches and instruction is offered at many places. Parasailing, which is now very popular, is available at a number of beaches, mostly on Zákynthos, as is jet-skiing.

WALKING

The islands not only have wonderful coasts but also beautiful interiors, much of them mountainous. There is some superb walking here and not all of it strenuous. The goal of more serious hikers will be the summit of Mount Énos (the highest peak in the Ionians), best tackled from the saddle between it and Mount Roúdi. There are companies that conduct walking tours of the islands, for interesting trips to Kefaloniá contact Trek Adventures (tel: 01789 868002; www.trek-adventures.co.uk). Serious botanists will find the hills of the islands a delight, and there are tailor-made botanical walking holidays available.

HORSE RIDING AND CYCLING

These are both excellent ways of seeing the islands. On Kefaloniá the Bavarian Horse Riding Stables, in Koulouráta about 6km (4 miles) south of Sámi, offers trips from one to seven days on horseback into the mountains and along the coast (tel: 6977 533203; www.kephalonia.com). The mountainous nature of the terrain makes cycling hard work but

Horse riding on Kefaloniá

extremely rewarding. Many of the minor roads are very quiet but take great care on the precipitous main coast roads.

EXCURSIONS BY KAÏKI

Popular boat trips on Zákynthos are to the Blue Caves at Cape Skinári (take the kaïki from the lighthouse at the cape, ignoring the touts at Ágios Nikólaos) and to Navágio Beach. There is also a plethora of all-day trips round the island. Take your pick from the harbour of Zákynthos Town.

ENVIRONMENTAL VOLUNTEERS

One of the most satisfying ways of seeing the islands is to volunteer on an environmental protection programme run by one of the local eco-groups. On Zákynthos much of the work is dedicated to safeguarding the nesting loggerhead turtles on

---

⊘ YACHTING

The relatively calm and safe waters around Zákynthos and Kefaloniá, coupled with the wonderful marine environment, have made this area very popular with yacht owners and companies running bareboat charter and flotilla holidays. On Kefaloniá the most popular harbour is Fiskárdo in the north of the island. However, this can get very busy, especially with novice crews being instructed through loudhailers by their group leader on the quayside. If you are after a little more peace and quiet then you would be better advised to head down the coast to Agía Efimía or along the spectacular west coast to the pretty horseshoe harbour of Ássos. Companies that charter boats and run flotillas include Sunsail (www.sunsail.com) and Nautilus (www.nautilusyachting.com).

The waters around Zákynthos and Kefaloniá attract yachting enthusiasts

Laganás Bay and to protecting the environment of the National Marine Park.

Several organisations are involved in this; the park authority itself is setting up a voluntary scheme (see their website www.nmp-zak.org for details), but the longest-standing organisation on Zákynthos is the Sea Turtle Protection Society of Greece (www.archelon.gr), which runs turtle protection programmes and other ecological activities.

On Kefaloniá, visitors under 25 years old can apply to take part in FNEC's (Fiskárdo's Nautical and Environmental Club) environmental protection programmes. As well as carrying out marine research work, they also run a network of volunteers to protect the feral ponies of Mount Énos.

SHOPPING

Prices are rising in Greece, and as a result you shouldn't expect great bargains on either Zákynthos or Kefaloniá. In souvenir and gift shops you might find that some good-natured bargaining is tolerated if you are buying more than one item or spending a reasonable amount, but don't push your luck. Local profit margins have to cover not only the tourist months but also the off season, when most shops are closed.

If you are not a resident of the EU, you might be able to claim back the 23 percent VAT (sales tax) included in the price of most goods, if you spend over a certain amount. Ask for details at shops with 'Tax-Free for Tourists' stickers.

WHAT TO BUY

Truth be told, Zákynthos and Kefaloniá are not a shoppers' paradise and the best things to buy as gifts or mementos of your trip are perishables, such as olive oil, thyme honey and local wines (see page 101). Among the tourist merchandise peddled in the resorts, from inflatable turtles and novelty key rings to mass-produced figurines, you'll have to look hard to find anything worth bringing home. An exception to this is jewellery, in gold and silver, which can be of very good quality and made in attractive, unusual designs. Zákynthos Town is a good place to look: try either Savvas (tel: 26950 23688) or Platinum (tel: 26950 25044), both of which are on Platía Agíou Márkou. In Argostóli most of the jewellers are along Lithóstroto. Note that the more upmarket the resort (for example, Fiskárdo), the more inflated the price of the jewellery is likely to be.

Another item worth looking out for is a decent reproduction icon. These can be skilfully executed and are widely available, but the best ones tend to be on sale at museums and monasteries.

Leather items, especially bags and sandals, can be good buys but you might want to shop around for the best quality and selection.

Ceramics are among the few artisanal items worth bringing home and the islands have some excellent craft potters, particularly in the attractive smaller villages. You may also consider buying hand-embroidered textiles; the women's cooperative in Volímes, Zákynthos, has an excellent reputation.

NIGHTLIFE

There are considerable differences in the nightlife on the two islands. For the most part, nightlife on Zákynthos falls into two broad types: that which is more traditionally Greek, ranging from the authentic (*kandádes* evenings in tavernas; see page 14) to the heavily tourist-orientated ('Greek nights'), and that revolving around the clubs in the resorts.

If the latter is your thing, then head for Laganás on Zákynthos, which has many nightclubs, including Rescue Club, Greece's largest club outside Athens. Other places to

Dining out in Fiskárdo

check out include Zeros and the Cameo Club, which is on the small island of Ágios Sóstis, accessible across a walkway from the beach. Elsewhere on Zákynthos, the clubs outside Argási are pretty lively, while those in Tsiliví and Alykés are a little more staid.

Kefaloniá's nightlife is generally more low key and, in Argostóli, revolves around the cafés and bars on Platía Valiánou and Lithóstroto, although the only proper club is Bass. Elsewhere on the island, apart from in the more lively resorts of Lássi and Skála, nightlife is focused on local bars or tavernas.

GREEK NIGHTS

Whichever resort you are staying in on Zákynthos, you will almost certainly come across a 'Greek Night', which generally comprises a fairly traditional meal, music (usually live) and dancing. It is, of course, the last that everyone comes to see. Traditional Greek dances are taught at an early age, and the dancers – be they specially hired performers, restaurant staff or simply locals who want to do their bit – can almost always be relied on for an energetic performance.

Whereas some Greek island dances are a little staid, Zakynthian males revel in athletic, fast dances with high-kicking, Cossack-like steps and not a little bravado. Dancing in a ring of fire is quite typical. Another dance involves picking up a glass of wine with the mouth (no hands allowed) from a press-up position. The wine is downed with a jerk of the neck. Another crowd pleaser is the solo *zimbékiko*. The spectators, clapping in time to the music, cheer on the dance. By the end of the night, it is a fair bet that the dancers will have cajoled everyone up on to the floor to join in a version of the *syrtáki*, Greece's best-known group dance; the steps are simplified for visitors.

A musician plays a handmade bouzoúki

These dances are usually all accompanied by the famous eight-stringed lute, the *bouzoúki*, which for many foreigners has become synonymous with all Greek music. In fact, the instrument (which is of Middle Eastern origin) is a comparatively recent import to the island, though the haunting melodies of Manos Hadjidakis and Mikis Theodorakis have made it an intrinsic part of Greek folklore.

CHILDREN

It is easy to travel with a family in Greece, and Zákynthos in particular is a popular destination for those with children. The Greeks are very tolerant of children – it is common to see local youngsters late at night in tavernas, eating and running around, and visitors' children will be accepted doing the same. In addition, many of the larger and more expensive hotels and resorts have facilities for children, including play areas and dedicated, shallow swimming pools. Children will be more than happy to visit the Zante Water Village (Sarakinádo; www.zantewatervillage.gr; open May–Aug), a waterpark with a variety of waterslides, swimming pools, Jacuzzis and even a go-kart circuit.

Many of the activities already mentioned are suitable for children and the active, outdoor life should appeal greatly to those with an adventurous spirit, with the beach being the obvious focus of activities. Do remember, however, that the Mediterranean sun is very strong and that children can burn easily and quickly. Make sure they wear a T-shirt and use a high-factor sunscreen.

On Zákynthos there are two 'toy trains' that might appeal to children. One runs frequently to and from Zákynthos Town to Argási, and another goes from Alykés in a circle through the nearby countryside, passing through Katastári and Pigadákia. Trekking on horseback is also a possibility (see page 87), though this is not one for very young children.

Beach-based activities are a hit with the kids

Activities centred around wildlife can also be popular. Trips to see the turtles (see page 88) and visits to the two natural history museums (see pages 36 and 75) are possible excursions that will go down well with the kids.

CALENDAR OF EVENTS

1 January New Year's Day (*Protohroniá*). Feast Day of Ágios Vasílis (St Basil). Before Western ideas of Santa Claus became widespread in Greece, this was the traditional day on which gifts were exchanged. Children go from house to house singing the traditional *kálanda*.

6 January Epiphany (*Agía Theofánia or Fóta*). In seaside parishes the priest or bishop blesses the waters by throwing a crucifix into the sea, then young men dive to retrieve it.

Easter The great festival of the Greek year. A moveable feast comprising several parts: **February**, *Apókries*, the period before Lent that is Greece's carnival season; **Clean Monday**, the first day of Orthodox Lent (*Katharí Deftéra*), when in good weather everyone goes out for a picnic; **Good Friday**, biers (*epitáfii*) from many churches are taken on a procession; **Easter Sunday**, at midnight on the Saturday the priest announces *Hristós Anésti* (Christ has risen) and passes the flame of life from the altar to the candles of the congregation. There then follow fireworks and noisy celebrations with music and dance.

25 March Independence Day.

1 May May Day. Workers' parades and excursions to the countryside to gather flowers and greenery for May wreaths.

3 May Feast of Agía Mávra, Maherádo, Zákynthos.

21 May Ionian Union Day (*Énosis ton Eptanison*) marks the anniversary of the seven islands joining the modern Greek state in 1864.

15 August Assumption of the Virgin Mary (*Apokímisis tis Panagías*), celebrated most bizarrely in the village of Markópoulo, Kefaloniá, by a 'snake festival' (6–15 August).

16 August Feast day of Ágios Gerásimos, patron saint of Kefaloniá (also 20 October).

24 August Feast day of Ágios Dionýsios (patron saint of the island), Zákynthos Town (also 17 December).

28 October *Óhi* Day. Celebration of the Greek refusal in 1941 to accept Mussolini's ultimatum, triggering their heroic resistance of Italy's invasion.

25 December Christmas Day.

EATING OUT

In general, Greek food is delicious, fresh and well prepared. Traditionally, a restaurant *(estiatório)* does not have entertainment; it is a place for straightforward eating. These often provide *magireftá*, oven-cooked dishes that you choose by entering the kitchen and indicating what you want. Tavernas, traditionally open only at night, are more social establishments where customers may spend an entire evening drinking and eating; *psarotavérnes* specialise in fish and seafood. A *psistariá* has rotary and flat grills for cooking meats and poultry.

MEZÉDES AND SALADS

Mezédes are small plates of food, akin to starters. They can be used in combination to make up whole meals. Common *mezédes* include: olives; *tzatzíki* (yoghurt dip flavoured with garlic, cucumber and mint); *taramosaláta* (fish-roe paste blended with breadcrumbs); *melitzanosaláta* (aubergine salad); *gígandes* (broad beans in tomato sauce); and *dolmádes* (vine leaves stuffed with rice and spices). *Kalamarákia tiganitá* are pieces of deep-fried squid (this is usually frozen, not fresh); *tyropitákia* are small pastry parcels filled with cheese; *keftédes* are small, fried meatballs flavoured with coriander and spices; and *saganáki* is a slice of cheese coated in flour and fried. The standard Greek salad of tomato, cucumber,

Some like it hot

Greek food is served lukewarm and with lots of olive oil, thought of as good for the digestion. For hot food, ask for it *zestó*; food without oil is *horís ládi*. However, both these requests will be considered eccentric.

Zákynthos beach bar

pepper, olives and feta cheese *(horiátiki saláta)* is a fine staple. *Maroúli* is lettuce, at its best as a finely shredded salad with spring onions and dill. Also popular, are various cold or luke-warm salads of boiled wild greens *(hórta)*.

MAIN COURSES

Common dishes include *mousakás* (minced meat, aubergine and tomato with béchamel sauce and a cheese topping), brought to Greece by refugees from Asia Minor, and *pastítsio* (macaroni and minced meat with béchamel sauce). *Kléftiko* is lamb, slowly baked until it is very tender, and *stifádo* is braised beef or rabbit with pearl onions. *Briám* (potatoes, tomatoes and courgettes) and *fasolákia laderá* (green beans and tomato sauce) are two other popular casserole dishes, while *fasoláda* (bean soup) is a winter favourite. A treat, if you can find them, are *anginάres* (artichokes); *bámies* (okra) are also particularly good.

Souvláki, a Greek classic

Meats grilled on a small skewer are known as *souvláki*, while *gýros* are thin slices of meat cut from a spit and served with salad on pitta bread. *Biftéki*, fried minced meat mixed with bread and spices, is ubiquitous. *Giouvétsi* is beef or lamb, pasta and tomato cooked in a pot. *Soutzoukákia* are rolls of minced meat cooked in tomato sauce. *Giouvarlákia* are rolls of minced meat covered in egg-and-lemon sauce (*avgolémono*). For more unusual foods you may encounter *kokorétsi* (lamb's offal wrapped in intestines and grilled over a spit), *myaló* (fried sheep brains), or sheep testicles, known as 'unmentionables' (*amelétita*). *Pátsas* is tripe, served up in a spicy soup, much vaunted as a hangover cure. If you are in Greece at Easter, try the tasty *magirítsa*, a soup made from finely chopped lamb's offal.

Desserts are not usually on the menu but often offered on the house with the bill: those you are most likely to encounter include yoghurt with honey, often with walnuts, and two kinds of *halvá*. *Halvá tis rínas* is a semolina cake and the compact *halvá tou bakáli*, the grocer's *halvá*, is made of flour, tahini, oil, honey and nuts. Sometimes you will find *galaktoboúreko*, filo pastry filled with custard and soaked in syrup, and *baklavás*, made of crushed nuts in filo pastry with syrup. In the summer, particularly late summer, don't miss the abundant grapes, figs, melon and watermelon.

LOCAL DISHES

There are a number of specialities that come from the two islands, some of which bear testimony to their history of invasion and occupation. On Zákynthos there is a strong tradition of home jam-making (known as *marmeláda*, from the English marmalade), although you will be lucky to find any outside of private houses. There is much influence from Italy across the Ionians, and this is seen in dishes such as *sofríto*, lightly fried veal with garlic and vinegar; *bourthíto*, a peppered fish stew; *biánco*, white fish stew with garlic; and *pastitsáda*, a spicy meat, macaroni and cheese dish. *Pantséta*, found on Zákynthos, is very similar to the Italian cured pork pancetta.

⊙ PSAROTAVÉRNES

These can be very expensive but will have some fresh fish unless winds have kept the boats in harbour. Fresh fish is sold by weight (before it is cleaned) and you might want to keep an eye on the scales, also look out for fish marked *katapsygméno* (frozen), sometimes just 'kat' or 'k'. Fish sizes vary from the tiny whitebait (*marídes*) and smelt (*atherína*), to the larger dentex (*synagrída*), swordfish (*xifías*) or grouper (*rofís*). In between are the smaller red mullet (*barboúni* or *koutsomoúra*) and several breams (*tsipoúra*, *fangrí*, *sargós* and *lithríni*). Cod (*bakaliáros*), salted or fresh, as well as *galéos*, a kind of shark, is common. Grilled octopus (*htapódi*) and cuttlefish (*soupiá*) are delicious, and deep fried squid (*kalamarákia*), usually frozen, is often available. You may also find lobster (*astakós*), usually boiled, but sometimes cooked with spaghetti.

Kefaloniá has its *kreatópita*, a pie consisting of meat and rice flavoured with cinnamon and topped with a thick pastry. This is available almost everywhere, while rather more unusual is the octopus pie traditionally eaten during Lent. You may also come across boiled goats' meat on Kefaloniá.

An Ionian quirk is *aliáda*, essentially the same as the garlic purée found elsewhere in Greece (where it is known as *skordaliá*) but made with potatoes rather than bread. Also look out for delicious, local *kolokythákia* (courgettes) boiled whole and served with vinegar. Local cheeses are worth trying anywhere, and those made from sheep's milk are often excellent, though many of the harder ones can be very strong and salty.

Both islands have excellent thyme honey, sold by the wayside in large jars, but this is not the only sweet speciality. Zákynthos produces a very sweet nougat called *mandoláto*, made from almonds and honey. *Amygdalópita* (almond pie) is a speciality of Kefaloniá, where you will also find *kydonópasto*, a quince paste similar to the Spanish *membrillo*.

WHAT TO DRINK

In the summer you will need to drink a lot of water, but do try to steer clear of bottled 'spring' water, as Greece's mountain of plastic bottles

Thyme honey from Kefaloniá

is growing ever higher. Tap water is perfectly safe on both Zákynthos and Kefaloniá, though it is extremely hard. If you carry your own water bottle, cafés and restaurants you visit will be happy to fill it for you. Better still, find one of the islands' well-regarded springs, from which locals often take their own drinking water.

Greece has delicious bottled fizzy lemonade *(lemonáda)*, which, unlike some other 'lemon drinks', does actually contain lemon juice; the best brands are Loux and IVI (HBH). Another drink worth looking out for is *soumáda*, a diluted orgeat syrup made from barley and almonds. Beer is widely available, the most likely offerings being Amstel and the more palatable Heineken; however, the local brand, Mythos, produced by the Boutari company, is one of the best.

Greece has been making wine for millennia and, although in the past some of its wines have been particularly esteemed, few are now well known outside the country. Kefaloniá is one of the best wine-producing islands and is particularly noted for whites made from the Robola grape, given an Apellation of Superior Quality. The vines grow well in the dry, stony soils common on the island, and it is possible to visit a number of the best wineries (see pages 62 and 65). Other major grape varieties include Muscat, used for a very fine sweet wine, and Mavrodaphne, which produces a strong red. Zákynthos also has a few good wines (see page 36), and its own cultivar, Zakynthino.

Local barrelled wines can be surprisingly good and are always worth a try. Resinated wine *(retsína)* can also be good, particularly when served very cold. *Oúzo*, a grape distillate with added aniseed oil, is drunk as an aperitif with water. *Tsípouro* is a clear, fiery grape distillate similar to the Italian *grappa*.

TO HELP YOU ORDER...

Is there a table available, please? **Ypárhi éna trapézi eléfthero, parakaló?**

I'd like a/some... **Tha íthela éna, mía/meriká...**

The bill, please. **To logariasmó, parakaló.**

BASIC FOODS

aláti salt
avgá eggs
kremídia onions
ládi (olive) oil
makarónia pasta
méli honey
pipéri pepper
psomí bread

rýzi rice
skórdo garlic
tyrí cheese
voútyro butter
xýdi vinegar
giaoúrti yoghurt
záhari sugar

MEZÉDES

andzoúyes anchovies
dolmádes stuffed vine-leaves
eliés olives
fava split peas
kolokithákia fried
tiganitá courgettes
loukánika sausages

melitzánes tiganités fried aubergines
saganáki fried cheese
spanakopita spinach pie
taramosaláta fish-roe dip
tyropitákia cheese pies
tzatziki yoghurt with garlic

MEAT

arní lamb
biftéki minced meat cake
brizóla chop
hirinó pork
keftédes meatballs

kotópoulo chicken
kréas meat
moshári veal/beef
sta kárvouna grilled
sto foúrno roast

soutzoukákia meatballs

souvlaki spit-roast

FISH

bakaliáros salt cod
barboúnia red mullet
frésko fresh
garídes prawns
htapódi octopus
kalamarákia squid

katapsygméno frozen
marídes whitebait
mýdia mussels
psári fish
sardéles sardines
soupyés cuttlefish
xifías swordfish

FRUIT AND VEGETABLES

angináres artichokes
arakás peas
domátes stuffed
gemistés tomatoes
fasólia haricot beans
hórta greens
horiátiki 'Greek salad'
kolokithákia courgettes
karpoúzi watermelon
maroúli lettuce
lemóni lemon
patátes potatoes
(tiganités/sto foúrno) (chips/roast)
piperiés stuffed
yemistés peppers
portokáli orange
saláta salad
stafýlia grapes

sýka figs
veríkoka apricot

Horiátiki, the classic Greek salad

PLACES TO EAT

The following prices reflect the average cost of a two-course meal (per person) and a half litre of wine. At all restaurants an automatic tax of 23 percent (VAT) is always included in the prices listed on the menu. It is customary to leave an additional five to 10 percent for the waiter, especially if they are an employee and not the owner. Most town restaurants are open year round but those in the resorts and villages only from May to October.

€€€ over 28 euros
€€ 17–28 euros
€ below 17 euros

ZÁKYNTHOS

Zákynthos Town

Akrotiri Taverna €€ *Akrotíri, 4km (2.5 miles) north of Zákynthos Town, tel: 26950 45712.* A pleasant summer-only taverna with a large garden. Grilled meats are a speciality but staff also bring round large trays of tempting *mezédes* from which you pick and choose. Prices are reasonable, and the house wine is more than acceptable.

Komis €€€ *Bastoúni tou Agíou, tel: 26950 26915,* www.komis-tavern. gr. A lovely psarotavérna tucked into a rather unlikely spot behind the port authority building (opposite Agíou Dionysíou). The emphasis is on rather pricey but fresh and inventive fish and seafood dishes, but there is a good list of *mezédes*, good wine and, better still, tempting desserts.

Malanos € *Agíou Athanasíou 38, Kípi district (south of the river off Kalamáki road), tel: 26950 45936.* A deservedly popular and inexpensive all-year shrine of *magireftá*, mince-rich *youvarlákia* and *fasolákia yahní* are typical offerings. There's also unusually good bread as well as the expected barrel wine. Often has live *kandádes* at weekends.

Prosilio €€€ *A. Panton and A. Latta 15, tel: 26950 22040*, www.prosilio zakynthos.gr. Located next to the central Platía Solomoú, this stylish modern restaurant serves traditional Greek fare with a creative twist, such as lamb with Jerusalem artichokes and goat's cheese, and a selection of fine wines. Its lovely garden is an additional attraction.

Vasilikós and Laganás Bay

Agnandi Taverna €€ *beyond Argási, 8km (5 miles) from Zákynthos Town, tel: 26950 35183*. An attractive modern wooden building on a steep slope overlooking the sea. It is slightly touristy, but the home cooking is authentic and tasty. The menu covers the generic standards, but also has some interesting specials.

Apelati € *1km (0.5 miles) east of Kerí, tel: 26950 43324*. This lovely rural tavern, tucked behind a field off the main road, offers a simple selection of wholesome country dishes from fresh meat and fish to delicious salads, much of it made from home produce.

Dennis €€ *Lithákia, tel: 26950 51387*, www.dennistaverna.com. A bit of an institution, and open all year round, Dennis's is a friendly, family-run long-standing taverna with a great atmosphere, serving a wide range of traditional food. Try the *mezédes* and meat from the charcoal grill – the pork chops are legendary; the house wine isn't bad either. There is also free transport back to your villa or hotel should you need it.

Kerí Lighthouse Restaurant €€€ *Kerí village, tel: 26950 43384*. The lighthouse taverna is well worth a visit, even if you just plan on ordering a drink and gazing at the Kerí Caves from above and admiring the sea views. The food is enjoyable, yet slightly on the expensive side.

Sarakina € *2km (1.2 miles) west of Laganás, tel: 26950 51606*. Set in a rambling old house with outdoor terraces amidst the olive groves, this evening-only taverna offers a huge range of quality local food and wine, as well as traditional music, popular with Greeks and tourists alike. It is well-advertised in Laganás and a free minibus comes round regularly to shuttle diners back and forth.

Theodoritsis €€ *just past Argási in Vasilikós municipal territory, tel: 26950 48500*. Theodoritsis is where the beau monde of Zákynthos go for a weekend blowout; the stress is on *magireftá*, but grills and *mezédes* are also available. Moderately pricey. Summer terrace overlooking town and tasteful interior. Open all year.

To Triodi €€ *Gérakas, tel: 26950 35215*. Lovely garden taverna next door to the Turtle Information Centre, where you can enjoy a variety of filling meat and fish dishes or smaller salads and snacks before a dip at the fantastic beach.

Zakanthi €€ *Kalamáki, tel: 26950 43586, www.facebook.com/zakanthi*. This is probably the most attractive place to eat in Kalamáki, dining in a large well-maintained garden. The food, which is quite good, is a mix of pasta, pizza and the usual Greek offerings (grills and salads). Once the sun has gone down and the subdued lighting comes on in the garden, it is lovely here.

The north

Cross Tavern €€ *Kambí, mobile: 30697 3334560*. A family-owned restaurant with an unbeatable location and amazing sea views. Freshly cooked traditional local fare at reasonable prices. Live Greek music on some days.

Kaki Rahi €€ *Pigadákia, tel: 26950 83580*. This restaurant offers a decent range of *magireftá*, grills and *mezédes*, served on a leafy terrace beside a running stream, from which the taverna gets its name. The local wine served here is excellent too.

Mikro Nisi €€ *Kokkínos, 1km (0.6 miles) beyond Makrýs Gialós, mobile: 30697 3050680, www.mikronisi.com*. Reasonable taverna food – *horiátiki, kalamarákia, souvláki* and the like – served in a delightful setting. The taverna is perched on the edge of a small headland overlooking a tiny harbour and you can watch the boats come and go as you eat.

Pilarinos € *Makrýs Gialós, tel: 26950 31396*. Set on a small hill just above this small but pleasant beach, this summer taverna offers a tasty range of grilled meat and fish, plus plenty of salads and dips.

Porto Limnionas €€ *Pórto Limniónas, near Ágios Léon, tel: 26957 72072*. Location can count for a lot, and this restaurant has one of the best on the island. The food is reasonably priced, standard taverna fare, plus some less common *mezédes* and pricier fish dishes, all served on a promontory overlooking an idyllic rocky bay. To cap things off, the restaurant faces west, so is a great place to watch the sun set.

Porto Roulis €€ *Kypséli Beach, near Drosiá, tel: 26950 61628*. A friendly place overlooking the sea and a narrow beach – and popular with islanders – Rouli's gets very fresh fish (one of its main attractions) but also has a good line in the usual Greek salads and vegetables. The house wine is drinkable, and the freshness of all the ingredients make a trip here well worth the detour off the main road.

KEFALONIÁ

Argostóli

There are a few places on or just off Platía Valianoú that are good for breakfast, a snack or for simply sitting with a drink. **Premier**, between Hotel Aenos and the Ionian Plaza, advertises itself as a *crêperie-gelaterie* but is not a bad place for breakfast or lunch (even if the service is very slow). Also nice is **Delakafe**, just up the hill at Sotiros 23, a small quiet place with good coffee, fresh juice and snacks. Of the cafés surrounding the square, **Le Sapin Noir** (tel: 26710 26240) is one of the most pleasant.

Captain's Table €€€ *A. Trítsi near main square, tel: 26710 27170*, www.captainstablerestaurant.com. Relocated to sleek modern premises on the seafront, this institution still serves hearty traditional dishes, with live *kandádes* on Saturday and every night in the season.

Casa Grec €€ *Metaxa Stavrou 10, tel: 26710 24091*. Mouth-watering value for money Mediterranean fare served in a charming ambiance. Stuffed Portobello mushrooms and the chef's special of chicken fillet with prawns are really worth a try.

Kyani Akti €€€ *A. Trítsi 1, far north end of the quay, tel: 26710 26680*. A superb *psarotavérna* built out over the sea. The speciality is, unsurprisingly, fresh fish and seafood, and they often have unusual things to try (including sea urchins and the delicious *dáktylia* – 'fingers' – which are akin to razor clams). All the fish and seafood is sold by weight (you go and pick it from the buckets at the back), but there is also a range of meat, *mezédes* and salads, plus excellent house wine.

Portside Taverna €€ *Metaxa 58, tel: 26710 24130*. The friendly Portside Taverna (inevitably overlooking the port) has a lot to offer, including excellent seafood dishes, surprisingly good wine and agreeable service.

To Arhontiko €€ *Rizospáston 5, tel: 26710 27213*. This compact, friendly taverna has seating on a small outside patio, from which you can hear the *kandádes* sung at the adjacent Captain's Table, whilst paying considerably less for tasty fare such as *exohikó* (baked lamb) or veal in tomato sauce. The *mezédes* and wine are excellent too.

Tzivras €€ *V. Vandorou 1, mobile: 30697 4735749*. Classic old-fashioned *estiatório*, only open until late afternoon but great for oven-baked dishes like *mousakás*, *Kefalonian kreatópita*, *gemistá* and *briám*.

Lixoúri and the south

Akrogiali € *Lixoúri quay (Andréa Laskarátou), towards south end, tel: 26710 92613*. An enduring, budget-priced institution, with largely local clientele. Wholesome and tasty food with a stress on oven-casserole food (including *giouvétsi*, *kreatópita* and great *hórta*), but also fish and grills in the evening, plus excellent bulk wine.

Blue Sea €€€ *Káto Katélios, tel: 26710 81122*. The fish here is fresh, sourced from the little anchorage adjacent, and superbly cooked. Budget on over €30 each for a large dinner including a share of *mezédes* and their bulk wine.

Dolphins Restaurant €€ *Sámi waterfront, tel: 26740 22008.* A basic but pleasant waterfront place, the best of an uninspiring bunch, with daily *magireftá* such as *briám* (similar to ratatouille), *giouvétsi* and good *hórta*. There is also fresh fish on offer, usually small tasty offerings including sardines, octopus and *marídes*.

Fotis Family €€ *Póros, tel: 26740 72972.* Set in a delightful position, built into the headland at the end of the town beach. Here, you eat on a first-storey balcony, which has views over the sea to Itháki. The menu focuses on a large range of fresh fish (priced by weight), but there are also good *mezédes* and salads.

Ksouras €€ *Petaní, Lixoúri peninsula, tel: 26710 97458.* Right in the middle of one of the island's best beaches and run by a welcoming Greek-American woman, this is a great spot for sunset dining. Grills and fish are the specialities, as well as salads and some *magireftá*.

Lorraine's Magic Hill €€ *Lourdáta, tel: 26710 83140*, www.lorrainesmagic hilllourdas.com. Perched on a hillside just above the beach, this gem run by the very friendly American lady it is named after, dishes up huge portions of traditional fare such as roast goat and *giouvétsi*. Great place for a cocktail too.

The north

Acqua Alaties Beacj €€ *Alaties Beach*, https://en-gb.facebook.com/ Acqua.Alaties.Beach. Situated on the rocky shore overlooking the sandy bay, this restaurant serves Greek classics as well as a selection of *mezédes* and salads. This is the perfect setting for a refreshing cocktail whilst watching the sun go down.

Agia Paraskevi €€€ *Agía Paraskeví, between Sámi and Agía Efimía, tel: 26740 23061.* A lovely spot from which to watch the waves break on the rocks below the huge terrace. The standard range of salads, *mezédes* and grilled meat and fish is available but the real speciality is the superb seafood marinara, bulging with fresh mussels and shrimp. You can dance it off in the adjacent Del Mare nightclub.

Amalia €€ *round headland from Agía Efimía harbour, tel: 26740 61088.* Here you can enjoy a range of *mezédes* such as *saganáki* or *loukánika*, or some heartier main dishes on a terrace overlooking the sea.

Lagoudera €€ *Fiskárdo, tel: 26740 41275.* Authentic restaurant with one branch on the harbour of Fiskárdo, the other just around the corner by the small square. Specialities include tasty home-style baked food, as well as fish, grilled meat and all the usual *mezédes*.

Makis € *Vasilikiádes, tel: 26740 51556.* You can enjoy a wonderful, inexpensive and extremely authentic meal in the large courtyard of this inland village establishment. There are succulent grills like lamb chops, as well as fine *mezédes* such as *kolokythokeftedes* (cheesy courgette patties).

Nefeli-Anait €€ *Ássos, tel: 26740 51251,* www.nefeli-anait.com. One of four establishments overlooking the very attractive harbour, this all-purpose taverna offers the usual range of salads and a few grilled and oven dishes, as well as fresh fish by the kilo. There is good barrelled wine and a selection of other drinks. If this place is too crowded, try the popular and more authentic **Estiatorio Platanos** on Platía Parísion behind the waterfront, set around a large tree.

Odisseas €€ *Agía Ierousalím, tel: 26740 41133.* A true hidden gem. You are assured a warm welcome and relaxed dining experience from the owner, while mum churns out the grub. All their ingredients are organic or free range and you can sample delights such as olive bread, slow-cooked lamb and ultra-fresh salads, all washed down with the fine house wine. They also have homemade honey, jam and other produce for sale.

Tassia €€€ *Apolitos wharf, Fiskárdo, tel: 26740 41205,* www.tassia.gr. A nice harbourfront spot with lovely views of Itháki. Established in 1972, this was the first restaurant to open in Fiskárdo. Acclaimed Greek chef Tassia Dendrinou offers traditional Kefalonian dishes cooked in a creative way. Seafood is a must here, especially octopus in wine, but can get very pricey. There is also an extensive wine list.

To Foki € *at the head of Fókis Bay, tel: 6944 757032.* This is a very pleasant and friendly taverna, situated just opposite the beach. It serves simple but tasty food – *fáva*, *souvláki* and salads – and lovely *milópita* (apple pie). Much better, and far cheaper, than anything to be found in Fiskárdo just down the road. Take mosquito repellent for the evenings.

Vasso's €€€ *southeast end of quay, Fiskárdo, tel: 06740 41276.* Magireftá with a difference: olive tapenade for your bread, dill and other herbs flavour many of the dishes, and there is seafood pasta and creative desserts. Reasonable (for *Fiskárdo* anyway) at about €30 each if you stay away from lobster and other more expensive types of fish.

A–Z TRAVEL TIPS

A SUMMARY OF PRACTICAL INFORMATION

A

ACCOMMODATION

Many hotels are heavily booked from mid-June until mid-September, especially during the first three weeks of August when reservations are strongly recommended. The decline in numbers in recent years means you should find a room on spec or via a travel agency on either island. On Kefaloniá, you can ask at the Tourist Information Office in Argostóli (see under Tourist Information).

Prices are controlled according to a rating system, based on a building's age, facilities, amenities and other factors. Hotels are rated from A to E (rooms in categories A and B have private bathrooms), but prices can vary widely within each category. Luxury establishments, rated L, are not price-controlled. A star system, designed to replace the letter scheme, was introduced in 2003 but is still not universally applied. The equivalents are roughly as follows:

Luxury – 5 stars
A – 4 stars
B – 3 stars
C – 2 stars
D and E – 1 star

In high summer some form of air conditioning will enable you to get a good night's sleep. If your room doesn't have air conditioning (and some older properties don't), there will either be a ceiling fan or you might be able to borrow a fan from reception or the owner.

Villas and apartments. There are many villas, apartments and studios (the latter terms are interchangeable) in Zákynthos and Kefaloniá available to rent. Accommodation ranges from simple rooms to lavishly appointed summer homes – sometimes tastefully converted from a traditional house or houses – complete with a swimming pool.

In the UK, companies offering top-of-the-range secluded luxury villas on Zákynthos and Kefaloniá are: Ionian & Aegean Island Holidays, tel: 020 8459 0777, www.ionianislandholidays.com; Greek Sun Holidays, tel: 017 3274 0317, www.greeksun.co.uk; Thomson, tel: 01732 740317, and Sunvil (Greek Islands Club), tel: 020 8568 4499, www.sunvil.co.uk.

Rooms in private homes. The cheapest rooms are those that are privately rented in people's homes, but these are becoming increasingly rare. They are almost always clean, and are graded A and B by the local tourist police, though rates are usually negotiable.

> I'd like a single/double room with bath/shower **Tha íthela éna monóklino/díklino me bánio/dous**
> What's the rate per night? **Póso éhi/stihízi gia káthe vrádi?**

AIRPORTS

Zákynthos: Located about 5km (3 miles) from Zákynthos Town, this busy airport has spacious arrivals and departures areas and all the necessary facilities. If you book through a tour operator you will be met at the airport and whisked off to your villa or resort, otherwise you will have to take a taxi into town (around €14–15). For information on flight arrivals and departures tel: 26950 29500, www.greek-airports.gr/zakinth.htm.

Kefaloniá: The airport is near the village of Miniá, about 7km (4 miles) south of Argostóli. The building is modern, with a few basic facilities such as a shop and refreshment stand, but like all island airports it can get very busy during high season. If you are not being met by a tour representative or are picking up a hire car booked in advance, then you have no option but to take a – costly – taxi into town (about €15–20). For information on arrivals and departures tel: 26710 29900, www.kefaloniaairport.info.

B

BICYCLE AND MOTORCYCLE HIRE

You can hire bicycles, motorcycles and quad bikes in all the tourist centres. However, many package operators warn clients against motorised cycles and scooters for the quite legitimate fear of an accident (and to drum up more business for organised excursions). It is vital that you check that motorbike hire does not invalidate your holiday insurance. Scooter hire is cheap (you should be quoted a rate per day, including third-party insurance and CDW collision-damage waiver). Terms vary by operator. Usually, to hire a motorbike with an engine larger than 50cc you must be at least 18 years old and hold a full motorcycle licence. It is illegal to ride without a crash helmet, or to drive without an appropriate licence on your person; on the spot fines approach €300.

It is certainly not advisable to ride a motorbike in shorts or a swimsuit, since burns or scrapes resulting from even a slight accident could be appalling. Inspect brakes and tyres before hiring and drive with care. Even on good roads there are occasional potholes.

Bicycle hire is less common, largely because of the mountainous terrain, but on Kefaloniá a good place for serious riders to seek information is the bike shop at the far (non-pedestrianised) end of Lithóstroto.

BUDGETING FOR YOUR TRIP

Greece is certainly not a budget destination these days, although the financial crisis has kept prices competitive. Consequently, it is still possible not to spend a fortune on Zákynthos and Kefaloniá, especially if you book an airfare/accommodation package. Otherwise, independent travellers can find return flights for around £100–200, decent places to stay from around €60–70 per night for a double room, with big discounts available out of the high season.

Eating out is considerably cheaper if you stick to *magireftá* and simple grills and *mezédes* in places frequented by locals: generally a three-course meal plus drinks in a decent restaurant or taverna will cost around €15–25 per person. Public transport and museum fees are inexpensive.

C

CAR HIRE

Unless visiting the islands with the intention of walking or cycling, you might consider hiring a car, especially on Zákynthos, where the bus service is very patchy. As elsewhere in Greece, car hire is not particularly cheap, but it is certainly less expensive than touring by taxi. Car hire starts from about €30 per day in low season (with a €500 excess on insurance for damage). For a decent family-sized car in high season, you should budget around €250 per week; all have air conditioning these days.

You'll find car-hire firms throughout the islands, especially in tourist centres. To be on the safe side, reserve a car ahead of time, especially for the high season. Local firms generally charge slightly less than international agencies and provide equally good cars and service. International chains that operate on the islands, bookable through their websites, include Avis, Budget, Europcar, Hertz, National, Sixt and Thrifty.

You will usually need a credit card for the deposit and a full national licence (held for at least one year) from your country of residence. If you are from a non-EU country, it is also mandatory to have an international driving permit. Depending on the model and the hire company, the minimum age for hiring a car varies from 21 to 25. Third-party liability insurance (CDW) is usually included in the stated rate, but with an excess amount, so it is always worth paying a little more for comprehensive coverage.

> What's the hire charge for a full day? **Póso kostízi giá mía méra?**
> I'd like to hire a car (tomorrow) **Tha íthela na nikiáso éna avtokínito (ávrio)**

CLIMATE

July and August are the sunniest, hottest and busiest tourist months. You may prefer to visit between mid-May and late June or from early September to mid-October. It can rain at any time of year, even in July and August. The Ionians are the greenest of all the Greek island chains. In winter it rains very hard. November and December are the wettest months and January the coldest, but even during these mid-winter doldrums the climate is temperate. Spring, when the islands burst with wild flowers, is the best time for walking.

The chart below shows each month's average air and sea temperature in Celsius and Fahrenheit, and the average number of hours of sunshine per day.

	J	F	M	A	M	J	J	A	S	O	N	D
Air												
°C	10	10	12	15	19	24	27	26	23	19	15	12
°F	50	50	54	59	66	75	81	79	73	66	59	54
Sea												
°C	15	15	15	16	18	21	24	25	24	21	19	18
°F	59	59	59	61	64	70	75	77	75	70	66	64
Sunshine hours												
	5	6	7	7	9	10	11	12	9	6	4	3

CLOTHING

Clothing is invariably casual on the islands. However, the Greeks do like to dress up when they go out in the evening and visitors who make a bit of an effort will be smiled upon. With regard to comfort, choose lightweight cotton clothing in spring and summer, and a warm jacket, sweater and rainwear in autumn and winter. Since it rains from time to time (outside of July and August), a protective coat or umbrella might be a good idea. Plastic or 'trekking' sandals are extremely useful for stony beaches; these are usually available in some shape or form from beach-side tourist shops.

CRIME AND SAFETY (SEE ALSO EMERGENCIES AND POLICE)

The Zakynthians and Kefalonians are, like the vast majority of Greek people, scrupulously honest. However, unfortunately, thefts occur, so it's sensible to leave valuables in the hotel safe. Take care of your passport but at the same time be aware that you're required to have official ID on your person at all times in Greece.

Possession of drugs is a very serious matter in Greece, carrying a stiff mandatory sentence. Make sure you have a prescription from your doctor if you will be carrying syringes, insulin, any narcotic drugs or even codeine, which is illegal in Greece.

D

DRIVING

Road conditions. Zákynthos has a reputation for having some of the most dangerous roads in Greece, so be very careful. The surfaces on main roads are generally very good, though curves in the road are often indicated too late, are sometimes unsignposted and are never banked. If there is a mirror on a bend, slow down to a low gear, it is probably going to be extremely tight or narrow, or perhaps both.

On many clifftop roads it is very dangerous to pass, so be patient if there is a slow-moving bus or heavy vehicle in front of you. Conversely, try to let local speed maniacs pass you as soon as it is safe to do so.

The secondary roads are some of the narrowest on any of the Greek islands – it's difficult to safely exceed 50kph (31mph) – while anything marked 'unsurfaced' on a map can be very rough indeed. Rockslides are common in the rainy season, and broken shoulders or potholes are not unknown on even the best-paved stretches. Drive with extreme caution, as you might be responsible for damage sustained to the underside of your hire car, even with comprehensive coverage.

Driving regulations. Drive on the right side and pass on the left. Traffic from the right has right of way. A Greek practice to be aware of is that if a driver flashes the lights, it means 'Stay where you are, I'm coming through', not 'Go ahead'. Seat belts are obligatory, as is the carrying of your driving licence while at the wheel; there is an €200 on the spot fine if you are caught without it. The speed limit is 80kph (50mph) inside built-up areas, 100kph (62mph) outside. In practice, however, the winding roads usually set the speed limit.

Are we on the right road for...? **Eímaste sto sostó drómo gia...?**
Fill the tank please, with (unleaded) petrol **Parakaló, gemíste tin me amólivdi**
My car has broken down **To avtokínito mou éhi halási**
There's been an accident **Égine éna atíhima**

Fuel. Generally you will never be far from a filling station, though in parts of the north and west of Zákynthos, and the north and centre of Kefaloniá, they are few and far between. Note that in rural areas filling stations are open only until about 7pm and closed on Sunday.

Detour Παράκαμψη/**Parákampsi**
Parking Παρκιγκ/**Párking**
No parking Απαγορεύεται/**Apagorévete to párking**
Be careful Προσοχή/**Prosohí**
Bus stop Στάση λεοφορείου/**Stási leoforíou**
Pedestrians Για πεζούς/**Gia pezoús**
Danger Κίνδυνος, επικίνδυνος/**Kíndinos, epikíndinos**
No entry Απαγορεύεται η είσοδος/**Apagorévete i ísodos**

On busy main roads and in resorts they open daily from early until late.

If you need help. For breakdown and accident assistance phone the Greek motoring club (ELPA), tel: 104 or 157, which has a reciprocal arrangement with most other national motoring associations. Some car-hire companies have agreements with other roadside emergency companies, such as Hellas Service (tel: 1057).

Road signs. On main roads and at junctions these will be in Greek and Latin (Western) letters; on secondary roads they may just be in Greek (for some important ones see the list).

E

ELECTRICITY

Greece has 220-volt/50-cycle AC current. Sockets are two-pin, so bring an adapter or transformer with you as necessary.

> a transformer **énas metashimatistís**
> an adapter **énas prosarmostís**

EMBASSIES AND CONSULATES

There is a United Kingdom consular office in Zákynthos Town.

British Honorary Vice Consulate: Fóskolou 28, Zákynthos Town; tel: 26950 22906.

Embassies (*presvía*) or consulates (*proxenío*) of all major countries are located in Athens.

Australia: Level 2, Hatziyiánni Méxi 5, tel: 21087 04000, www.greece. embassy.gov.au.

Canada: Ethnikis Antistaseos 48, Chalandri, tel: 21072 73400, www. international.gc.ca/world-monde/greece-grece/athens-athenes. aspx/lang=eng.

Ireland: Vassiléos Konstantínou 7, tel: 21072 32771, www.embassy ofireland.gr.

New Zealand: Kifissías 76, tel: 21069 24136, www.mfat.govet.nz/en/ embassies.

South Africa: Kifissías 60, tel: 21061 06645.

UK: Ploutárhou 1, tel: 21072 72600, http://ukingreece.fco.gov.uk.

US: Vassilísis Sofías 91, tel: 21072 12951, http://athens.usembassy.gov.

EMERGENCIES

Police: (all-purpose emergency number) **100**; (Zákynthos Town) 26950 22100; (Argostóli) 26710 22200.

Tourist Police: 1571; (Zákynthos Town) 26950 27367; (Argostóli) 26710 22815.

Hospitals: (Zákynthos Town) 26950 59100; (Argostóli) 26710 24641.

Ambulance: 166; (Zákynthos Town) 26950 23166.

Fire: 199.

Vehicle emergency: 104 or **157**.

Port Authority: (Zákynthos Town) 26950 28117; (Argostóli) 26710 22224.

G

GETTING THERE

It is possible to cross Europe overland and take the ferry from Italy to Pátra on the Greek mainland and then a ferry to either Sámi on Kefaloniá, or, from Kyllíni, further down the coast, to Zákynthos Town. From the UK you can fly directly into both Zákynthos and Kefaloniá on easyJet, www.easyjet.com from April to October. Out of season, you will have to fly to Athens first, from where there are daily domestic flights on Olympic (www.olympicair.com), Aegean (www.aegeanair.com) or Sky Express (www.skyexpress.gr) to both islands (45 minutes), or take the coach from the Kifissoú bus station (several daily to Zákynthos and Argostóli, around 7 hours; all coaches connect with ferries for which there is a small additional cost).

H

HEALTH AND MEDICAL CARE

In theory, EU citizens with a European Health Insurance Card (obtainable in their own country) can get free treatment under the Greek health service. However, you are likely to receive the minimum treatment; medication must be paid for and state hospital facilities are over-stretched in the tourist season. It's therefore best to obtain private medical insurance. British citizens should check new healthcare regulations post-Brexit. Doctors and dentists are concentrated in Zákynthos Town and Argostóli; your hotel or apartment owner can find you one who speaks English. Most resorts have a local medical clinic.

Hospitals. The hospitals in Zákynthos Town and Argostóli operate a 24-hour emergency service (tel: 166, or, Zákynthos: tel: 26950 59100; Argostóli tel: 26710 24641). Otherwise call the tourist police (Zákynthos tel: 26950 27367; Argostóli tel: 26710 22815).

Pharmacies. A red or green cross on a white background identifies a pharmacy (*farmakío*). They are normally open only during the morning Monday to Friday but a notice on the door should tell you the nearest one for after-hours service. One pharmacy is always open in Zákynthos Town and Argostóli at night and on Saturday and Sunday. Without a prescription, you can't get sleeping pills, barbiturates or medicine for stomach upsets.

While swimming look out for sea urchins – their black spines

a doctor/dentist **énas giatrós/odontoíatros**
hospital **nosokomío**
an upset stomach **varystomahiá**
sunstroke **ilíasi**
a fever **pyretós**

are very sharp and will break off in your skin. If this happens, seek medical attention, as they are very tricky to remove.

L

LANGUAGE

Only in remote countryside spots is it possible for non-Greek-speaking tourists to run into serious communication problems. You will find that basic English is spoken almost everywhere. Stress is a very important feature of the Greek language, denoted by an accent above the vowel of the syllable to be emphasised. The table lists the Greek letters in their upper- and lower-case forms, followed by the closest individual or combined letters to which they correspond in English.

Α α	a	as in cat
Β β	v	as in English
Γ γ	g	as in go (except pronounced 'y' before 'e' and 'i'sounds)
Δ δ	d	like th in this
Ε ε	e	as in get
Ζ ζ	z	as in English
Η η	i	as in ski
Θ θ	th	like th in thin
Ι ι	i	as in ski
Κ κ	k	as in English
Λ λ	l	as in English
Μ μ	m	as in English
Ν ν	n	as in English
Ξ ξ	x	as in exercise
Ο ο	o	as in fox

Π π	p	as in English
Ρ ρ	r	as in English but rolled more
Σ σ/ς	s	as in English, except sounds like z before m or g sounds
Τ τ	t	as in English
Υ υ	y	as in country
Φ φ	f	as in English
Χ χ	h	as in Scottish loch
Ψ ψ	ps	as in tipsy
Ω ω	o	as in fox

M

MAPS

The best maps available of Zákynthos and Kefaloniá are published by Orama Editions. They are clear and accurate and give place names in both Greek letters and in transliteration.

These maps are available locally from Stanfords in the UK (www.stanfords.co.uk). Free tourist maps of lesser quality are widely available on the islands.

MEDIA

Newspapers and magazines *(efimerídes; periodiká)*. During the tourist season, foreign-language newspapers are on sale at shops and kiosks on the island, generally on the day after publication.

Television *(tiliórasi)*. Most hotels and many bars offer satellite television networks, including CNN, BBC World and, in some of the busier resorts, Sky.

Radio. BBC World Service is no longer broadcast on short wave but can be streamed on www.bbc.co.uk. Note that live sports events cannot be broadcast.

MONEY

Currency *(nómisma)*. In common with most other Western European countries, the euro (EUR or €) is the official currency used in Greece. Notes are in denominations of 5, 10, 20, 50, 100 and 500 euros; coins are 1 and 2 euros and 1, 2, 5, 10, 20 and 50 cents.

Banks and currency exchange. You'll find banks in Zákynthos Town, Argostóli and in the larger resort areas. Hotels and travel agencies (the latter sometimes called 'tourist offices') are authorised to change money, but you will probably get less for your money than you would from a bank.

ATMs. The easiest method to obtain cash is through 'hole-in-the-wall' cash dispensers. These can be found in Zákynthos Town, Argostóli and in all of the larger resorts. Depending upon your own individual card fees, this might also be the cheapest way to get money.

Credit cards *(pistotikés kártes)*. The major credit cards are accepted in many shops and by car-hire firms, most hotels, more expensive restaurants and some (but not all) filling stations. Be aware that you might have to pay an additional 5 to 7 percent for the privilege of using plastic.

> I want to change some pounds/dollars **Thélo na allákso merikés líres/meriká dollária**
> Can I pay with this credit card? **Boró na pliróso me aftí tin pistotikí kárta?**

O

OPENING TIMES

The siesta (the traditional Mediterranean early afternoon break) is still alive and well on Zákynthos and Kefaloniá, and observed most strictly outside tourist areas.

Shops. Traditional hours are generally Mon–Sat 8.30 or 9am–2 or

2.30pm. On Tuesday, Thursday and Friday shops reopen in the evening from 5.30 or 6pm until 8.30–9pm. Shops catering to tourists often stay open through the siesta and until late each evening in the summer, as well as part of Sunday. Larger supermarkets open Mon–Fri 8.30am–8.30pm and Sat 9am–6pm.

Museums and tourist attractions. State-run museums are closed on Monday. Museums are typically open Tue–Sat 8.30am–3pm and Sun 8.30 or 9.30am–2.30 or 3pm.

Banks. Mon–Thu 8am–2.30pm and Fri 8.30am–2pm.

Businesses and offices. 8am–1pm, then 2–5pm. Government offices work 8am–1.30pm, sometimes 2.30pm, and don't reopen.

Restaurants and tavernas. More traditional establishments open for lunch from noon until around 3.30pm and for dinner from 7pm to 11.30pm or later.

P

POLICE

Emergency telephone number: **100**.

Tourist police: Zákynthos, tel: 26950 27367

Argostóli, tel: 26710 22815

The tourist police (*touristikí astynomía*) have a specific mission to help visitors to the island, as well as to accompany state inspectors of hotels and restaurants to ensure that proper standards and prices are maintained.

Traffic police check car documents and driving licences, operate speed traps and issue fines for illegal parking (fines in Greece are high). Car-hire companies will use your credit-card details to pay ignored parking tickets; you have 10 working days to pay moving violations in person. Failing that, a court date will be set, and a summons sent to your home address. Failure to appear will result in an extra conviction for contempt of court, and make future re-entry to Greece extremely difficult.

Where's the nearest police station? **Pou íne to kondinótero astynomikó tmíma?**

POST OFFICES

Post offices (ELTA) handle letters, parcels and money orders but no longer exchange foreign currency. Look for a blue sign with the head of Hermes traced on it in yellow.

Post offices are generally open Mon–Fri 7.30am–2pm. Registered letters and parcels to non-EU destinations are checked before being sent, so don't seal them until presenting them at the desk. The main post office in Zákynthos Town is on Tertséti (Mon–Fri 7.30am–4pm), in Argostóli it is found on Lithóstroto (open as above).

Letterboxes are yellow but if there are two slots, make sure you use the one marked *exoterikó* (abroad). In tourist hotels, the receptionist will take care of dispatching your mail.

Have you received any mail for...? **Éhete grámmata giá...?**
a stamp for this letter/postcard **éna grammatósimo giaftó to grámma/giaftí tin kart postál**
express (special delivery) **katepígon**
registered **systiméno**

PUBLIC HOLIDAYS

Banks, offices and shops are closed on the following national holidays, as well as during some feasts and festivals (see also the Calendar of events on page 95):

1 January *Protohroniá* New Year's Day
6 January *Ágia Theofánia* Epiphany
25 March *Ikostipémpti Martíou (tou Evangelismoú)* Greek Independence Day

1 May Protomagiá May Day

15 August *Dekapendávgoustos* (tis Panagías) Assumption Day

28 October *Ikostiogdóïs Oktovríou Óhi* ('No') Day, celebrating defiance of the 1940 Italian ultimatum

25 December *Hristoúgenna* Christmas Day

26 December *Sýnaxi Theotókou* Meeting of Virgin's Entourage

Moveable dates:

Katharí Deftéra 1st day of Lent: 'Clean Monday'

Megáli Paraskeví Good Friday

Páscha Easter Sunday

tou Agíou Pnévmatos Whit (Pentecost) Sunday and Monday ('Holy Spirit'), June

Note: These moveable holidays are celebrated according to dates in the Greek Orthodox calendar, which usually differ from Catholic or Protestant dates.

R

RELIGION

The national religion of Greece is Greek Orthodox.

As elsewhere in southern Europe, you must dress modestly to visit churches and monasteries, which normally means long trousers for men, a long skirt or trousers for women and covered shoulders for both sexes. However, men are often allowed to wear long shorts and skirts may be provided at the back of churches for women to wrap around themselves.

T

TELEPHONES

Local calling. There are no longer any area codes as such in Greece; even within the same local-call zone you must dial all 10 digits of the number. What were the old codes are now merely the locators: 26950

for all of Zákynthos; 26710 for Argostóli, Lixoúri and the southwest; and 26740 for the east coast and north from Póros to Fiskárdo, plus the island of Itháki.

From overseas. To call Greece from abroad, first dial the international access code (00 from the UK), then **30** (the country code for Greece) and finally all 10 digits of the local number.

Long distance from Greece. International direct dialling is available at street-corner phone booths. These take phonecards (*tilekártes*), which are quite good value. Pre-paid VoIP calling cards with a free-phone access code and scratch-off PIN number are becoming more common; they can be used from any phone and are by far the cheapest way to call abroad. To reverse charges (collect calls), dial 151 for Europe and 161 for the rest of the world. Overseas directory assistance is through the international operator (dial 161). For the local operator, dial 132.

reverse-charge (collect) call **plirotéo apó to paralípti**

TIME ZONES

Greek time is GMT plus two hours. Daylight saving, when Greek clocks are put forward one hour, is observed from the last Sunday of March to the last Sunday of October. The chart shows the times in Greece and various other places during the European summer.

New York	London	Paris	**Greece**	Sydney	Auckland
5am	10am	11am	**noon**	8pm	9pm

TIPPING

The Greeks aren't obsessed with tipping, but it is the norm to leave a little more if service has been good. Usual amounts are as follows: hotel porter, €1 per bag; hotel maid, €1 per day; waiter, 5–10 percent; taxi driver, 10 percent; hairdresser/barber, 10 percent; lavatory attendant, €0.50.

TOILETS

Public conveniences are rare and best avoided. A better option is to use facilities at museums or the better cafés. If you do drop in specifically to use the toilet, it's customary to purchase coffee or some other drink before leaving.

Important note: you are always expected to put toilet tissue in the waste bin rather than down the toilet. Due to their narrow-bore pipes, toilets easily become clogged.

Where is the toilet? **Pou íne i toualétta?**

TOURIST INFORMATION

The national Visit Greece (www.visitgreece.gr; still sometimes known as the GNTO or EOT in Greek) has the following offices abroad:

UK and Ireland: 4 Great Portland Street, London W1W 8QJ; tel: 020 7495 9300.

US: 800 3rd Avenue, New York, NY 10022; tel: (212) 421 5777.

These offices supply general information and glossy pictures, but when it comes to anything specific on Zákynthos or Kefaloniá they are usually of little help.

Zákynthos, strangely, does not have an official (EOT) tourism office, but you could try asking the tourist police for information. The Kefaloniá office in Argostóli (open daily 8am–2.30pm; near the port authority; tel: 26710 22248) breaks the mould by being both helpful and informative. One recommended agency is Pama Travel in Fiskárdo, Kefaloniá (tel: 26740 41033, www.pamatravel.com).

TRANSPORT

Buses (*leoforía*). The public bus service on Zákynthos is patchy but, where it does exist, it is very good value. Timetables are displayed at bus stops (*stásis*) and at the KTEL bus station in Zákynthos Town (tel: 26950 22255/42656, www.ktel-zakynthos.gr), inconveniently located 2km up behind the centre. Most services run between Zákynthos Town and Laganás Bay and Vasilikós. For all buses, buy your tickets on board or from nearby kiosks. You can flag a bus down or disembark anywhere within reason.

The service on Kefaloniá is much better, making touring the island by public transport a real possibility. Direct buses run between Argostóli (on A. Trítsi, tel: 26710 22276, www.ktelkefalonias.gr) and all the other major towns (Póros, Sámi, Agía Efimía and Fiskárdo), and between Fiskárdo, Sámi, Póros and Skála. The Pallíki Peninsula is less well served but there is a service between Lixoúri and Xí. There is also a regular local service between Argostóli and Lássi. The fares are very reasonable and, generally, the service is frequent and punctual.

Taxis. These are an expensive way to get around but may be your only option in parts of Zákynthos. Make sure the meter is switched on; there are two rates depending on time of day and whether you are inside or outside town. Radio taxis can be summoned, for which there's a small surcharge.

Ferries. Regular ferries run between Pátra on the mainland and Sámi on Kefaloniá, and Kyllíni and Zákynthos Town. There are also services from Kyllíni to Póros on Kefaloniá and occasionally direct to Argostóli. There is also a ferry from Ágios Nikólaos (Skinári), in the north of Zákynthos, to the tiny port of Pesáda on Kefaloniá. A ferry runs between Sámi and Píso Aetós on Itháki. A new small express ferry links Zákynthos Town to Sámi and other Ionian Islands. For current ferry schedules and fares check with your nearest travel agent, the port authority (see under Emergencies) or online at www.openseas.gr.

> What's the fare to...? **Póso éhi éna isitírio giá...?**
> When's the next bus to...? **Póte févgi to epómeno leoforío giá...?**

V

VISAS AND ENTRY REQUIREMENTS

All EU citizens can enter Greece to visit or work for an unlimited length of time. Citizens of Ireland can enter with a valid identity card or passport. British citizens must be in possession of a valid passport. Entry conditions following Brexit may change, check before you travel.

Citizens of the US, Canada, Australia and New Zealand can stay for up to three months on production of a valid passport. South African citizens can stay for up to two months on production of a valid passport. No visas are needed for these stays. If you wish to extend these timescales you must obtain a permit from the proper department of either Zákynthos Town or Argostóli police stations.

Greece has strict regulations about importing drugs. All the obvious ones are illegal, and there are strong punitive measures for anyone breaking the rules. Codeine and some tranquillisers are also banned. If you take any drug on the advice of your doctor, carry enough for your needs in an official container, as medicines for personal use are permitted.

Since the abolition of duty-free allowances for all EU countries, all goods brought into Greece from Britain and Ireland must be duty-paid. In theory there are no limitations to the amount of duty-paid goods that can be brought into the country. However, cigarettes and most spirits are much cheaper in Greece than in Britain and Ireland (government duty is much lower, so waiting until you reach your destination to buy these goods will save you money).

For citizens of non-EU countries, allowances for duty-free goods brought into Greece are: 200 cigarettes or 50 cigars or 250g of tobacco; 1 litre of spirits or 4 litres of wine.

Non-EU residents can claim back Value Added Tax (currently between 6 and 24 percent) on any items costing over €120, provided they export the item within 90 days of purchase. Tax-rebate forms are available at tourist shops and department stores. Keep the receipt and form. Make your claim at the customs area of the airport when departing.

Currency restrictions. There are no limits on the amount of euros visitors can import or export. There are no restrictions on travellers' cheques, but cash sums of more than $10,000 or its equivalent should be declared on entry.

W

WEBSITES AND INTERNET ACCESS

Wi-Fi and internet cafés. As free Wi-Fi is now available at just about all accommodations and almost all cafés/restaurants, very few internet cafés remain and only in the two capitals.

There are now a number of useful websites for people travelling to Zákynthos and Kefaloniá:

www.visitgreece.gr The official site of the GNTO/EOT.

www.culture.gr The site of the Ministry of Culture, giving useful information on museums and archaeological sites.

www.openseas.gr An excellent site giving online timetables for most Greek ferry routes.

www.zanteweb.gr Pretty comprehensive site with a wealth of information on Zákynthos.

www.zanteisland.com Excellent site with information on Zákynthos.

www.kefalonia-island.gr Useful site devoted to Kefaloniá.

www.ithacagreece.com Excellent site giving all sorts of information, news and views of Itháki.

RECOMMENDED HOTELS

Although finding a room at short notice or on spec is not a problem for most of the summer, it is still wise to reserve well in advance for the peak season of the first three weeks in August. To telephone a hotel, dial the international country code for Greece (30), followed by the 10-digit number provided in our listings.

All hotels are classified by the Greek National Tourist Organization: luxury (L) class is at the very top, then A class down to E class (only hotels of L, A, B and C classes are featured below). In 2003, a star system (five-star equal to L, four-star to A, etc) was introduced but has been slow to catch on.

Rating establishes minimum price rates but prices can often vary widely within each class according to the season, location and availability of rooms. By law, rates must always be posted in all rooms; in practice this is often ignored.

The price categories below are for a double room with bath per night in high season, excluding the August super peak. All hotel room rates include VAT (Value Added Tax) of 23 percent. All L- and A-class hotels have air conditioning. Most hotels in beach resorts are only open from April or May to October, and quite often even less than this. Those in Zákynthos Town and Argostóli are open all year round.

€€€€	above 180 euros
€€€	120–180 euros
€€	80–120 euros
€	below 80 euros

ZÁKYNTHOS

Zákynthos Town

Hotel Alba €€ *Lámbrou Zivá 38, Zákynthos Town, tel: 26950 26641*, www.albahotel.gr. This small B-class hotel is located in a fairly quiet area just two blocks in from the seafront. Facilities include air conditioning, television in the rooms and room service.

Hotel Palatino €€€ *Kolokotróni 10 and Kolivá, Zákynthos Town, tel: 26950 27780*, www.palatinohotel.gr. A surprisingly good-value upmarket place. The rooms, designed for business travellers, have all the trimmings, and the hotel as a whole is well tended and professionally run. A buffet breakfast is provided, and there is also a restaurant.

Hotel Plaza €€ *Kolokotróni 2, Zákynthos Town, tel: 26950 45733*, www. plazazante.gr. Probably the best value hotel in town, in the quiet Repáro district, a short distance in from the town beach. The compact rooms have air conditioning and TV.

Hotel Strada Marina €€€ *Lombárdou 14, Zákynthos Town, tel: 26950 42761*, www.stradamarina.gr. The largest place in Zákynthos Town, with 112 comfortable but not overly exciting rooms. In a vast modern building on the seafront, so many of the rooms have great views of the harbour. Breakfast is included, and there is a rooftop pool.

Vasilikós and Laganás Bay

Levantino Studios & Apartments € *Kamínia beach, tel: 26950 35366*, www.levantino.gr. Ten quiet and attractive apartments close to the sea at the town end of the Vasilikós Peninsula. All are equipped with a kitchen, and some look out over the gardens and sea. Good discounts available out of high season.

Hotel Matilda €€ *Vasilikós district, tel: 26950 35376*, www.matildahotel. gr. A designer, B-class hotel on a hilltop, with commanding sea views from all its rooms and a large pool terrace.

Pansion Limni € *Límni Kerioú beach, tel: 26950 26289*, www.pan sionlimni.com. Welcoming and superb value pension just behind the far end of the beach. There are some larger, newer apartments a little further inland. Guests often receive home-made olive oil and wine.

Porto Koukla Beach Hotel €€€ *Lithakiá, tel: 26950 52393*, www.porto-koukla.com. This large hotel is situated at the western end of Laganás Bay. Popular mainly with German and Austrian visitors, Porto Koukla is well away from the tawdriness further east. The hotel gardens back on to a narrow beach, which is overlooked by the hotel's excellent and cheap taverna.

Sirocco Hotel €€ *Kalamáki, tel: 26950 26083*, www.siroccohotel.com. This is a good and reasonably quiet option in Kalamáki; the hotel's stylish standard rooms are a bargain out of season. There is a large swimming pool set in an attractive garden, and the beach is not too far away.

Vasilikos Beach €€ *Ágios Nikólaos, tel: 26950 35325*, www.hotelvasilikosbeach.gr. Large hotel with airy rooms that include all mod cons, a pool and a decent restaurant. The hotel also runs the popular water sports complex on the beach and arranges a free bus to bring people from Laganás and Kalamáki.

Villa Katerina € *Porto Roma, Vasilikós, tel: 26950 35456*, www.villakaterina.com. These two buildings, in pretty gardens, have simple rooms with kitchenettes and attached bathrooms. Set back from the beach the rooms are very quiet, and the surrounding area is lovely.

The north

Amoúdi Hotel € *Amoúdi, tel: 26950 62560*, www.amoudihotel.com. Tucked just inland from one of the nicer coves, between the busier resorts of Tsiliví and Alykés, this modern hotel offers spacious apartments, all with kitchenettes and balconies, and there is a fine pool.

Anenomilos (The Windmills) €€ *Korithí, Cape Skinári, tel: 26950 31132/31241*, www.potamitisbros.gr. One of the most attractive places to stay on Zákynthos. It consists of two converted windmills and some cheaper stone apartments at the very north end of the island. The friendly Potamitis family also run the excellent To Faros taverna and the cheapest trips to the nearby Blue Caves.

Anetis Beach Hotel € *Tsiliví, tel: 26950 28899,* www.anetishotel.gr. Compact but pleasant little place, set just back from the main beach in a lively but not noisy part of the resort. Many of the rooms have balconies facing the sea.

Ionian Star Hotel €€ *Alykés, tel: 26950 83416,* www.ionian-star.gr. A smallish and very well-kept hotel. The spotless rooms are excellent value (breakfast is included) and there is a restaurant which specialises in Greek food.

Louis Plagos Beach €€€€ *Aboúla Beach, Tsiliví, tel: 26950 62800,* www.louishotels.com. This is a large resort hotel with a huge range of facilities, particularly for children. The rooms are plain but large and have balconies, and there a good hotel pool and restaurant. Five day minimum stay.

Nobelos Seaside Lodge €€€€ *Ágios Nikólaos (Skinári), tel: 26950 31400,* www.nobelos.gr. This luxury spot in the north of the island is expensive but lovely. The four tastefully decorated suites are in a traditional stone-built house, each with individual character. Along with excellent service, breakfast is provided and there's a secluded bay for swimming close by.

Panorama € *Ágios Nikólaos (Skinári), tel: 26950 31013,* panorama-apts@ath.forthnet.gr. A modest but friendly hotel in its own grounds on a bluff just south of the village with cosy rooms, many affording sea views. Great value with simple breakfast included.

Plessas Palace €€ *Alikanás, tel: 26950 41480,* www.plessaspalace.com. The spacious rooms are decorated in warm colours and other facilities include a pool, mini market and even a library. Near the village centre, almost a kilometre from the beach.

Zante Palace € *Tsiliví, tel: 26950 49090,* www.zantepalace.com. This huge modern hotel is on the bluff overlooking Tsiliví Bay, giving great views across to Kefaloniá. For what's on offer the rooms (which look out over the bay) are good value, and there is a nicely situated pool.

KEFALONIÁ

Argostóli

Aenos Hotel €€€ *Platía Vallianoú, Argostóli, tel: 26710 28013,* www. aenoshotel.com. The uncluttered pastel-shaded rooms with large attached bathrooms probably give the Aenos the edge as the best place to stay on the town's central square; it is also marginally quieter. American buffet breakfast included.

Hotel Ionian Plaza €€€ *Platía Vallianoú, Argostóli, tel: 26710 25581,* www. ionianplaza.gr. Excellent-value, C-class, designer hotel, with modern bathrooms and balconies overlooking the palm-studded square. The rooms are a bit on the small side, but the staff are friendly. Open all year but 3-night minimum stay in summer.

Kefalonia Grand €€ *Andóni Trítsi 82, Argostóli, tel: 26710 24981,* www. kefaloniagrand.gr. Formally the Olga, this seafront property has been totally refurbished and reinvented as a surprisingly good value boutique hotel, with snazzily designed and comfortable rooms.

Oskars Studios & Apartments €€ *Fanari, Lassi Argostóli, tel: 26710 23438,* www.oskars.gr. A complex of 15 clean simply furnished rooms with kitchenettes. On-site restaurant. Open all year.

Lixoúri and the south

9 Muses €€€€ *Skála, tel: 26710 83563,* www.9museshotel.com. This is an attractively designed bungalow complex set in well-tended garden just above mid-beach, with the room interiors doing justice to the surroundings. Officially C-class but priced (and equipped) as B.

Captain's House Hotel € *Skala, tel: 26710 83389,* www.captainshouse. net. Friendly chocolate-coloured place with 28 rooms a couple of blocks from the resort's main street and not far from the beach. All rooms are air-conditioned, with balconies and fridges.

La Cité €€ *Lixoúri, tel: 26740 92701*, www.lacitehotellixouri.gr. Four blocks uphill from the harbour, the good-value hotel has tastefully and colourfully furnished rooms and a uniquely shaped pool in its lush, exotic gardens.

Lara € *Lourdáta (Paralía Lourdás), tel: 26710 31157*, www.lara.gr. A peaceful, family-run C-class hotel, set in an olive grove some 300m (330yds) up the access road to the long sandy beach.

Méditerranée €€€€ *Lássi, tel: 26710 28760*, www.mediterraneehotel.gr. A vast hotel behind a small strip of beach. Facilities include a pool, tennis courts, two restaurants and shops. The rooms are high quality but greatly overpriced.

Melissani €€ *Sámi, tel: 26740 22464*, www.melissanihotel.gr. Just uphill from the harbour, this friendly place is a tad old-fashioned but offers some of the most reasonably priced rooms on the island.

Odysseus Palace €€ *Póros, tel: 26740 72036*, www.kefalonia-hotel.gr. This attractive modern hotel is the most comfortable place to stay in town. Good discounts may be available for the large and airy rooms (studios and apartments). Being away from the seafront, the hotel is quieter than most. Open all year.

Panas Hotel €€€ *Platía Spartiá, tel: 26710 69941*, www.panas-kefalonia. com. A large but pleasant B-class hotel on Lourdáta Bay, close to a good beach. The rooms, all of which have a balcony, are fine, if a little unimaginative. The hotel does, however, have good facilities for children, including their own pool and play area. There are also a couple of restaurants and a poolside bar.

Santa Irena € *Póros, tel: 26740 72017, email:* maki@otenet.gr. Cosy hotel offering compact but bright and comfortable rooms at unbeatable prices. Quiet inland location, a few blocks from the seafront. Only open in high season.

Hotel Summery € *Lixoúri, tel: 26710 91771/91871*, www.hotelsummery. gr. A large but quiet hotel on Lixoúri's beach (to the south of town) that mainly caters to tour groups. The rooms are clean and unfussy, and some have balconies. For the amenities on offer (pool, plenty of sporty activities, and a shop) the prices are quite reasonable.

Tara Beach €€ *Skála, tel: 26710 83341/83250*, www.tarabeach.gr. A large but unobtrusive hotel on an excellent beach. The rooms are decent, and, if you can't be bothered to waddle the few metres to the sea, there is a good pool in the pleasant gardens, beside which is a handy bar.

Trapezáki Bay Hotel €€€ *500m above Trapezáki beach, tel: 26710 31502*, www.trapezakibayhotel.com. Smart upmarket resort with a full range of amenities, including pool, restaurant, bar and lavishly furnished rooms. The policy of maintaining one price all season makes it good value in high summer; airport transfer included.

The north

Agnantia Apartments €€€ *Tselendáta, Fiskárdo, tel: 26740 51801–2*, www.agnantia.com. Very well maintained and beautifully located (although a little way out of Fiskárdo), these new hillside rooms are a lovely place to stay. As well as friendly and efficient service, the rooms are tasteful and comfortable, with a small kitchen area, and most have a balcony with wonderful views over to Itháki. A good, and generous, breakfast is included.

Archontiko €€€ *Fiskárdo, tel: 26740 41342*, www.archontiko-fiskardo.gr. Splendidly converted stone mansion backing onto the harbour. The rooms are stylishly decorated and air-conditioned, with sparkling bathrooms. There are a couple of rooms overlooking the harbour but noise comes with the view.

Athina Beach Hotel €€ *Karavómylos, tel: 26740 22779*, www.athinahotel.gr. Barely 2km (1.2 miles) from Sámi, close to a fine beach, this is the best place to stay on the bay. There is a small pool, the rooms are spacious and well-maintained and service is good. Sizeable discounts out of high season.

Cosi's Inn €€ *Ássos, tel: 26740 51420*, www.cosisinn.gr. One of the few places to stay in Ássos and certainly the best value. The simple rooms are set around a small courtyard, up the hill from the harbour.

Emelisse Nature Resort €€€€ *Éblissi, near Fiskárdo, tel: 26740 41200*, www.arthotel.gr/emelisse. Expensive (A-class) but chic, this boutique hotel is set in a traditional building. The well-designed rooms have luxurious bathrooms, and, inevitably, the infinity pool has a lovely view. For this sort of money you should expect to be pampered, and the service lives up to expectations. Minimum stay is three nights.

Mina's Apartments € *Divaráta, tel: 26740 61515*, www.minasapartments.gr. Just above the main junction in Divaráta, these spacious and well-furnished studios and apartments with kitchenettes are easily the best of the limited accommodation options close to stunning Mýrtos beach.

Moustakis Hotel €€€ *Agía Efimía, tel: 26740 61060*. Small, and tucked away behind the harbourfront, this is the most pleasant hotel in town but rather overpriced. All the rooms have air conditioning and balconies. Breakfast is available (extra charge). Discounts available for long stays.

Panormos €€ *Fiskárdo, tel: 26740 41203*, anais_haritou@yahoo.com. If you are looking for somewhere central, these six very reasonably priced rooms are above a restaurant right on Fiskárdo's picturesque waterfront – worth the price for the location alone.

Regina's € *Fiskárdo, tel: 26740 41125*, www.regina-studios.gr. Simple but comfortable rooms at the back of the village, near the village's attractive car park. There is a shady courtyard and the family that runs the place is very hospitable. The best deal in this upmarket resort.

DICTIONARY

ENGLISH–GREEK

adj adjective   **adv** adverb   **BE** British English   **n** noun   **prep** preposition   **v** verb

A

access n πρόσβαση
prohz•vah•see

accessory αξεσουάρ
ah•kseh•soo•ahr

accident ατύχημα
ah•tee•khee•mah

accompany συνοδεύω
see•noh•THeh•voh

account n λογαριασμός
loh•ghahr•yahz•mohs

adaptor προσαρμοστής
proh•sahr•moh•stees

address n διεύθυνση
THee•ehf•theen•see

admission είσοδος ee•soh•Thohs
ee•soh•Thohs

adult n ενήλικας eh•nee•lee•kahs
eh•nee•lee•kahs

advance προκαταβολή
proh•kah•tah•voh•lee

after μετά meh•tah
meh•tah

afternoon απόγευμα
ah•poh•yehv•mah

after-sun lotion λοσιόν μετά
την ηλιοθεραπεία loh•siohn
meh•tah teen ee•lioh•theh•
rah•pee•ah

age n ηλικία eh•lee•kee•ah
eh•lee•kee•ah

agree συμφωνώ seem•foh•noh
seem•foh•noh

air conditioning κλιματισμός
klee•mah•teez•mohs

air pump n αντλία αέρος
ahn•dlee•ah ah•eh•rohs

airline αεροπορική εταιρία
_ah•eh•roh•poh•ree•kee
eh•the•ree•ah_

airmail αεροπορικώς
ah•eh•roh•poh•ree•kohs

airport αεροδρόμιο
ah•eh•roh•THroh•mee•oh

aisle seat διάδρομος
THee•ah•Throh•mohs

allergic αλλεργικός
ahl•ehr•yee•kohs

allergy αλλεργία ah•lehr•yee•ah
ah•lehr•yee•ah

alone μόνος moh•nohs
moh•nohs

aluminum foil αλουμινόχαρτο
ah•loo•mee•noh•khah•rtoh

amazing καταπληκτικός
kah•tahp•leek•tee•kohs

ambassador πρεσβευτής
prehz•vehf•tees

amber κεχριμπάρι
kehkh•reem•bah•ree

ambulance ασθενοφόρο
ahs•theh•noh•foh•roh

American adj αμερικάνικος
ah•meh•ree•kah•nee•kohs;
(nationality) Αμερικανός
ah•meh•ree•kah•nohs

amount n ποσό poh•soh
poh•soh

amusement park πάρκο
ψυχαγωγίας pahr•koh
psee•khah•ghoh•yee•ahs

animal ζώο zoh•oh
zoh•oh

another άλλος ah•lohs
ah•lohs

antibiotic αντιβιοτικό
ahn•dee•vee•oh•tee•koh

antiques store κατάστημα με
αντίκες kah•tah•stee•mah meh
ahn•tee•kehs

antiseptic cream αντισηπτική
κρέμα ahn•dee•seep•tee•kee
kreh•mah

anything οτιδήποτε

oh•tee•THee•poh•teh

apartment διαμέρισμα
THee•ah•meh•reez•mah

apologize ζητώ συγγνώμη
zee•toh seegh•noh•mee

appendix σκωληκοειδίτιδα
skoh•lee•koh•ee•
THee•tee•THah

appointment ραντεβού
rahn•deh•voo

architecture αρχιτεκτονική
ahr•khee•teh•ktoh•nee•kee

area code κωδικός
περιοχής koh•THee•kohs
peh•ree•oh•khees

arm n χέρι kheh•ree
kheh•ree

arrange κανονίζω
kah•noh•nee•zoh

arrest v συλλαμβάνω
see•lahm•vah•noh

arrive φτάνω ftah•noh
ftah•noh

art τέχνη tekh•nee
tekh•nee

art gallery γκαλερί τέχνης
gah•leh•ree tekh•nees

ashtray σταχτοδοχείο
stakh•toh•THoh•khee•oh

ask ζητώ zee•toh
zee•toh

aspirin ασπιρίνη
ahs•pee•ree•nee

asthmatic ασθματικός
ahsth•mah•tee•kohs

ATM ATM ehee•tee•ehm
ehee•tee•ehm

attack n επίθεση
eh•pee•theh•see; v επιτίθεμαι
eh•pee•tee•theh•meh

attractive ελκυστικός
ehl•kees•tee•kohs

authenticity αυθεντικότητα
ahf•thehn•dee•koh•tee•tah

B

baby μωρό moh•roh

baby food βρεφική τροφή
vreh•fee•kee troh•fee

baby seat καρέκλα μωρού
kah•reh•klah moh•roo

babysitter μπέιμπι σίτερ
beh•ee•bee see•tehr

back n πλάτη plah•tee

back ache πόνος στην πλάτη
poh•nohs steen plah•tee

backgammon τάβλι tah•vlee

bad κακός kah•kohs

baggage αποσκευές
ah•pohs•keh•vehs

baggage check φύλαξη
αποσκευών fee•lah•ksee
ah•poh•skeh•vohn

baggage reclaim παραλαβή
αποσκευών pah•rah•lah•vee
ah•poh•skeh•vohn

bakery αρτοποιείο
ah•rtoh•pee•ee•oh

balcony μπαλκόνι bahl•koh•nee

ballet μπαλέτο bah•leh•toh

bandage γάζα ghah•zah

bank τράπεζα trah•peh•zah

bank account λογαριασμός
τραπέζης loh•ghahr•yahz•mohs
trah•peh•zees

bank loan τραπεζικό δάνειο
trah•peh•zee•koh THah•nee•oh

bar μπαρ bahr

barber κουρείο koo•ree•oh

basket καλάθι kah•lah•THee

basketball μπάσκετ bah•skeht

bathing suit μαγιό mah•yoh

bathroom μπάνιο bah•nioh

battery μπαταρία
bah•tah•ree•ah

beach παραλία pah•rah•lee•ah

beautiful όμορφος oh•mohr•fohs

bed κρεβάτι kreh•vah•tee

bed and breakfast διαμονή με
πρωινό THiah•moh•nee meh
proh•ee•noh

bedding σεντόνια sehn•doh•niah

bedroom υπνοδωμάτιο
eep•noh•THah•mah•tee•oh

before πριν preen

beginner αρχάριος
ahr•khah•ree•ohs

belong ανήκω ah•nee•koh

belt ζώνη zoh•nee

bicycle ποδήλατο
poh•THee•lah•toh

big μεγάλος meh•ghah•lohs

bikini μπικίνι bee•kee•nee

bird πουλί poo•lee

bite n (insect) τσίμπημα
tsee•bee•mah

bladder ουροδόχος κύστη
oo•roh•THoh•khohs kee•stee

blanket κουβέρτα koo•veh•rtah

bleed n αιμορραγία
eh•moh•rah•yee•ah; v
αιμορραγώ eh•moh•rah•yoh

blinds περσίδες peh•rsee•THehs

blister φουσκάλα foo•skah•lah

blood αίμα eh•mah

blood group ομάδα αίματος
oh•mah•THah eh•mah•tohs

blood pressure πίεση pee•eh•see

blouse μπλούζα bloo•zah

boarding card κάρτα επιβίβασης
kah•rtah eh•pee•vee•vah•sees

boat βάρκα vahr•kah

boat trip ταξίδι με πλοίο
tah•ksee•THee meh plee•oh

body σώμα soh•mah

bone οστό oh•stoh

book n βιβλίο veev•lee•oh;
v κάνω κράτηση kah•noh
krah•tee•see

bookstore βιβλιοπωλείο
veev•lee•oh•poh•lee•oh

boot μπότα boh•tah

border (country) σύνορο
see•noh•roh

boring βαρετός vah•reh•tohs

borrow δανείζομαι
THah•nee•zoh•meh

botanical garden βοτανικός
κήπος voh•tah•nee•kohs
kee•pohs

bottle μπουκάλι boo•kah•lee

bottle opener τιρμπουσόν
teer•boo•sohn

bowel έντερο ehn•deh•roh

box office ταχυδρομική θυρίδα
tah•khee•THroh•mee•kee
THee•ree•THah

boxing n μποξ bohks

boy αγόρι ah•ghoh•ree

boyfriend φίλος fee•lohs

bra σουτιέν soo•tiehn

break n διάλειμμα THee•ah•
lee•mah; v σπάω spah•oh

breakdown n (car) βλάβη
vlah•vee

breakfast πρωινό proh•ee•noh

break-in n διάρρηξη
THee•ah•ree•ksee

breast στήθος stee•THohs

breathe αναπνέω
ah•nahp•neh•oh

breathtaking φαντασμαγορικός
fahn•dahz•mah•
ghoh•ree•kohs

bridge n (over water) γέφυρα yeh•
fee•rah; (card game) μπριτζ
breetz

briefcase χαρτοφύλακας
khah•rtoh•fee•lah•kahs

briefs (men's, women's) σλιπ
sleep (women's); κυλοτάκι
kee•loh•tah•kee

bring φέρνω fehr•noh

Britain Βρετανία
vreh•tah•nee•ah

British adj βρετανικός
vreh•tah•nee•kohs; (nationality)
Βρετανός vreh•tah•nohs

brochure φυλλάδιο
fee•lah•THee•oh

broken σπασμένος
spahz•_meh_•nohs

broom n σκούπα _skoo_•pah

browse ξεφυλλίζω
kseh•fee•_lee_•zoh

bruise n μελανιά meh•lah•_niah_

brush n βούρτσα _voor_•tsah; v βουρτσίζω voor•_tsee_•zoh

build κτίζω _ktee_•zoh

building κτίριο _ktee_•ree•oh

burn n έγκαυμα _eh_•gahv•mah

bus λεωφορείο
leh•oh•_ree_•oh

bus route διαδρομή λεωφορείων
THee•ah•_THroh_•mee
leh•oh•foh•_ree_•ohn

bus station σταθμός
λεωφορείων stahTH•_mohs_
leh•oh•foh•_ree_•ohn

bus stop στάση λεωφορείου
stah•see leh•oh•foh•_ree_•oo

business class μπίζνες θέση
bee•znehs _theh_•see

business trip επαγγελματικό
ταξίδι eh•pah•gehl•mah•tee•
koh tah•_ksee_•THee

busy (occupied)
απασχολημένος
ah•pahs•khoh•lee•meh•nohs

but αλλά ah•_lah_

butane gas υγραέριο
eegh•rah•_eh_•ree•oh

butcher shop κρεοπωλείο
kreh•oh•poh•_lee_•oh

button κουμπί koo•_bee_

buy αγοράζω ah•ghoh•_rah_•zoh

C

cabaret καμπαρέ kah•bah•_reh_

cabin καμπίνα kah•_bee_•nah

cable car τελεφερίκ
teh•leh•feh•_reek_

cafe καφετέρια
kah•feh•_teh_•ree•ah

calendar ημερολόγιο
ee•meh•roh•_loh_•yee•oh

call collect με χρέωση του
καλούμενου meh _khreh_•oh•see
too kah•_loo_•meh•noo

call n κλήση _klee_•see; v καλώ
kah•_loh_

camcorder φορητή
βιντεοκάμερα foh•ree•_tee_
vee•deh•oh•_kah_•meh•rah

camera φωτογραφική μηχανή
foh•tohgh•rah•fee•_kee_
mee•khah•_nee_

camera case θήκη μηχανής
thee•kee meh•khah•_nees_

camera store κατάστημα με
φωτογραφικά είδη kah•_tah_•
stee•mah meh foh•tohgh•
rah•fee•_kah_ ee•THee

camp bed κρεβάτι
εκστρατείας kreh•_vah_•tee
ehk•strah•_tee_•ahs

camping κάμπινγκ kah•mpeeng

camping equipment εξοπλισμός
κάμπινγκ ehk•sohp•leez•_mohs_
kah•mpeeng

campsite χώρος κάμπινγκ
khoh•rohs kah•mpeeng

can opener ανοιχτήρι
ah•neekh•_tee_•ree

Canada Καναδάς kah•nah•_THahs_

canal κανάλι kah•_nah_•lee

cancel v ακυρώνω
ah•kee•_roh_•noh

cancer (disease) καρκίνος
kahr•_kee_•nohs

candle κερί keh•_ree_

canoe κανό kah•_noh_

car αυτοκίνητο
ahf•toh•_kee_•nee•toh

car park [BE] χώρος στάθμευσης
khoh•rohs stahth•mehf•sees

car rental ενοικίαση αυτοκινήτων
eh•nee•_kee_•ah•see
ahf•toh•kee•_nee_•tohn

car wash πλύσιμο
αυτοκινήτου _plee_•see•moh
ahf•toh•kee•_nee_•too

carafe καράφα kah•_rah_•fah

caravan τροχόσπιτο
troh•_khohs_•pee•toh

cards χαρτιά khahr•_tiah_

carpet (fitted) μοκέτα
moh•_keh_•tah

carton κουτί koo•_tee_

cash desk [BE] ταμείο
tah•_mee_•oh

cash n μετρητά meht•ree•_tah_;
v εξαργυρώνω
eh•ksahr•ghee•_roh_•noh

casino καζίνο kah•_see_•noh

castle κάστρο _kahs_•troh

catch v (bus) παίρνω pehr•noh

cathedral καθεδρικός ναός
kah•theh•THree•_kohs_ nah•_ohs_

cave n σπήλαιο _spee_•leh•oh

CD σι ντι see dee

cell phone κινητό kee•nee•_toh_

change n αλλαγή ah•lah•_yee_; v
αλλάζω ah•_lah_•zoh

cheap φτηνός ftee•_nohs_

check n (bank) επιταγή eh•pee•
tah•_yee_; (bill) λογαριασμός
loh•ghahr•yah•z•mohs

choose διαλέγω THiah•_leh_•ghoh

clean καθαρός kah•thah•_rohs_

cling film [BE] διαφανή
μεμβράνη _THee_•ah•fah•nee
mehm•_vrah_•nee

clothing store κατάστημα
ρούχων kah•_tahs_•tee•mah
roo•khohn

cold adj (temperature) κρύος
kree•ohs; n (chill) κρυολόγημα
kree•oh•_loh_•yee•mah

collapse v καταρρέω
kah•tah•_reh_•oh

collect v παίρνω _peh_•rnoh

color n χρώμα _khroh_•mah

comb n χτένα _khteh_•nah; v
χτενίζω khteh•_nee_•zoh

come έρχομαι _ehr_•khoh•meh

come back v (return) επιστρέφω
eh•pees•_treh_•foh

commission n *(agent fee)* προμήθεια proh•<u>mee</u>•thee•ah
company n *(business)* εταιρία eh•teh•<u>ree</u>•ah; *(companionship)* παρέα pah•<u>reh</u>•ah
complain παραπονιέμαι pah•rah•poh•<u>nieh</u>•meh
computer υπολογιστής ee•poh•loh•yee•<u>stees</u>
concert συναυλία see•nahv•<u>lee</u>•ah
concert hall αίθουσα συναυλιών <u>eh</u>•thoo•sah see•nahv•lee•<u>ohn</u>
conditioner (hair) γαλάκτωμα για τα μαλλιά ghah•<u>lah</u>•ktoh•mah yah tah mah•<u>liah</u>
condom προφυλακτικό proh•fee•lah•ktee•<u>koh</u>
conference συνέδριο see•<u>neh</u>•THree•oh
confirm επιβεβαιώνω eh•pee•veh•veh•<u>oh</u>•noh
constipation δυσκοιλιότητα thees•kee•lee•<u>oh</u>•tee•tah
Consulate Προξενείο proh•kseh•<u>nee</u>•oh
consult ν συμβουλεύομαι seem•voo•<u>leh</u>•voh•meh
contact ν επικοινωνώ eh•pee•kee•noh•<u>noh</u>
contact fluid υγρό για φακούς επαφής eegh•<u>roh</u> yah fah•<u>koos</u> eh•pah•<u>fees</u>
contact lens φακοί επαφής fah•<u>kohs</u> eh•pah•<u>fees</u>
contagious μεταδοτικός meh•tah•THoh•tee•<u>kohs</u>
contain περιέχω peh•ree•<u>eh</u>•khoh
contraceptive pill αντισυλληπτικό χάπι ahn•dee•see•<u>leep</u>•tee•<u>koh</u> khah•pee
cook n *(chef)* μάγειρας <u>mah</u>•yee•rahs; ν μαγειρεύω mah•yee•<u>reh</u>•voh

copper χαλκός khahl•<u>kohs</u>
corkscrew τιρμπουσόν teer•boo•<u>sohn</u>
corner γωνία ghoh•<u>nee</u>•ah
correct ν διορθώνω THee•ohr•<u>thoh</u>•noh
cosmetics καλλυντικά kah•leen•dee•<u>kah</u>
cot [BE] παιδικό κρεβάτι peh•THee•<u>koh</u> kreh•<u>vah</u>•tee
cotton βαμβάκι vahm•<u>vah</u>•kee
cough n βήχας <u>vee</u>•khahs; ν βήχω <u>vee</u>•khoh
counter ταμείο tah•<u>mee</u>•oh
country (nation) χώρα <u>khoh</u>•rah
countryside εξοχή eh•ksoh•<u>khee</u>
couple n *(pair)* ζευγάρι zehv•<u>ghah</u>•ree
courier n *(messenger)* κούριερ <u>koo</u>•ree•ehr
court house δικαστήριο THee•kahs•<u>tee</u>•ree•oh
cramp n κράμπα <u>krahm</u>•bah
credit card πιστωτική κάρτα pees•toh•tee•<u>kee</u> <u>kahr</u>•tah
crib [cot BE] παιδικό κρεβάτι peh•THee•<u>koh</u> kreh•<u>vah</u>•tee
crown n *(dental, royal)* κορώνα koh•<u>roh</u>•nah
cruise n κρουαζιέρα kroo•ahz•<u>yeh</u>•rah
crutch n *(walking support)* δεκανίκι THeh•kah•<u>nee</u>•kee
crystal n κρύσταλλο <u>kree</u>•stah•loh
cup φλυτζάνι flee•<u>jah</u>•nee
cupboard ντουλάπα doo•<u>lah</u>•pah
currency νόμισμα <u>noh</u>•meez•mah
currency exchange office γραφείο ανταλλαγής συναλλάγματος ghrah•<u>fee</u>•oh ahn•dah•lah•<u>yees</u> see•nah•<u>lahgh</u>•mah•tohs
customs (tolls) τελωνείο teh•loh•<u>nee</u>•oh
customs declaration (tolls)

τελωνειακή δήλωση teh•loh•nee•ah•<u>kee</u> THee•<u>loh</u>•see
cut n *(wound)* κόψιμο <u>koh</u>•psee•moh
cut glass n σκαλιστό γυαλί skah•lees•<u>toh</u> yah•<u>lee</u>
cycle helmet κράνος ποδηλάτη <u>krah</u>•nohs poh•THee•<u>lah</u>•tee
cyclist ποδηλάτης poh•THee•<u>lah</u>•tees
Cypriot adj κυπριακός <u>keep</u>•ree•ah•<u>kohs</u>; *(nationality)* Κύπριος <u>kee</u>•pree•ohs
Cyprus Κύπρος <u>kee</u>•prohs

D

damage n ζημιά zee•<u>miah</u>; ν καταστρέφω kah•tah•<u>streh</u>•foh
dance ν χορεύω khoh•<u>reh</u>•voh
dangerous επικίνδυνος eh•pee•<u>keen</u>•THee•nohs
dark adj *(color)* σκούρος <u>skoo</u>•rohs
dawn n ξημερώματα ksee•meh•<u>roh</u>•mah•tah
day trip ημερήσια εκδρομή ee•meh•<u>ree</u>•see•ah ehk•THroh•<u>mee</u>
deaf κουφός koo•<u>fohs</u>
decide αποφασίζω ah•poh•fah•<u>see</u>•zoh
deck n κατάστρωμα kah•<u>tah</u>•stroh•mah
deck chair σεζ-λονγκ sehz <u>lohng</u>
declare δηλώνω THee•<u>loh</u>•noh
deduct *(money)* αφαιρώ ah•feh•<u>roh</u>
defrost ξεπαγώνω kseh•pah•<u>ghoh</u>•noh
degrees (temperature) βαθμοί vahth•<u>mee</u>
delay n καθυστέρηση kah•thee•<u>steh</u>•ree•see; ν καθυστερώ kah•thee•steh•<u>roh</u>

delicious νόστιμος
nohs•tee•mohs

deliver παραδίδω
pah•rah•THEE•THoh

dental floss οδοντικό νήμα
oh•THohn•dee•koh nee•mah

dentist οδοντίατρος
oh•THohn•dee•ah•trohs

deodorant αποσμητικό
ah•pohz•mee•tee•koh

department store
πολυκατάστημα
poh•lee•kah•tahs•tee•mah

departure (travel) αναχώρηση
ah•nah•khoh•ree•see

departure lounge αίθουσα
αναχωρήσεων *eh•thoo•sah
ah•nah•khoh•ree•seh•ohn*

depend εξαρτώμαι
eh•ksahr•toh•meh

deposit *n* (down payment)
προκαταβολή *proh•kah•
tah•voh•lee*

describe περιγράφω
peh•reegh•rah•foh

designer σχεδιαστής
skheh•THee•ahs•tees

detergent απορρυπαντικό
ah•poh•ree•pahn•dee•koh

develop (photos) εμφανίζω
ehm•fah•nee•zoh

diabetes διαβήτης
THee•ah•vee•tees

diabetic διαβητικός
THee•ah•vee•tee•kohs

diagnosis διάγνωση
THee•ahgh•noh•see

dialing code κωδικός
koh•THee•kohs

diamond *n* διαμάντι
THiah•mahn•dee

diaper πάνα μωρού *pah•nah
moh•roo*

diarrhea διάρροια
THee•ah•ree•ah

dice *n* ζάρια *zah•riah*

dictionary λεξικό *leh•ksee•koh*

diesel ντήζελ *dee•zehl*

diet *n* δίαιτα *THee•eh•tah*

difficult δύσκολος
THee•skoh•lohs

dining room τραπεζαρία
trah•peh•zah•ree•ah

dinner βραδινό *vrah•THee•noh*

direct *v* κατευθύνω
kah•tehf•thee•noh

direction *n* (instruction) οδηγία
oh•THee•yee•ah

dirty *adj* Βρώμικος
vroh•mee•kohs

disabled άτομο με ειδικές
ανάγκες *ah•toh•moh meh ee•
•nahn THee•kehs ah•gehs*

discounted ticket μειωμένο
εισιτήριο *mee•oh•meh•noh
ee•see•tee•ree•oh*

dishwashing liquid λίγο υγρό
πιάτων *lee•ghoh ee•ghroh
piah•tohn*

district περιφέρεια
peh•ree•feh•ree•ah

disturb ενοχλώ *eh•noh•khloh*

diving equipment
καταδυτικός εξοπλισμός
*kah•tah•THee•tee•kohs
eh•ksoh•pleez•mohs*

divorced διαζευγμένος
THee•ah•zehv•ghmeh•nohs

dock προκυμαία
proh•kee•meh•ah

doctor γιατρός *yah•trohs*

doll κούκλα *kook•lah*

dollar δολάριο *THoh•lah•ree•oh*

door πόρτα *pohr•tah*

dosage δοσολογία
THoh•soh•loh•yee•ah

double *adj* διπλός *THeep•lohs*

double bed διπλό κρεβάτι
THeep•loh kreh•vah•tee

double room δίκλινο
δωμάτιο *THeek•lee•noh
THoh•mah•tee•oh*

downtown area κέντρο της
πόλης *kehn•droh tees poh•lees*

dozen ντουζίνα *doo•zee•nah*

dress *n* φόρεμα *foh•reh•mah*

drink *n* ποτό *poh•toh*; *v* πίνω
pee•noh

drive *v* οδηγώ *oh•THee•ghoh*

drugstore φαρμακείο
fahr•mah•kee•oh

dry cleaner καθαριστήριο
kah•thah•rees•tee•ree•oh

dubbed μεταγλωττισμένος *meh•
tahgh•loh•teez•meh•nohs*

dusty σκονισμένος
skoh•neez•meh•nohs

duty (customs) φόρος
foh•rohs; (obligation) καθήκον
kah•thee•kohn

duty-free goods αφορολόγητα
είδη *ah•foh•roh•loh•yee•tah
ee•THee*

duty-free shop κατάστημα
αφορολόγητων *kah•tahs•tee•
mah ah•foh•roh•loh•yee•tohn*

E

each κάθε ένα *kah•theh eh•nah*

ear αυτί *ahf•tee*

earache πόνος στο αυτί *poh•nohs
stoh ahf•tee*

early νωρίς *noh•rees*

east ανατολικά
ah•nah•toh•lee•kah

easy *adj* εύκολος *ehf•koh•lohs*

eat τρώω *troh•oh*

economical οικονομικός
ee•koh•noh•mee•kohs

economy class τουριστική θέση
too•ree•stee•kee theh•see

elastic ελαστικός
eh•lahs•tee•kohs

electrical outlet πρίζα *pree•zah*

e-mail ηλεκτρονικό ταχυδρομείο
*(e-mail) ee•lehk•troh•nee•koh
tah•hee•dro•mee•oh
(ee•meh•eel)*

embassy πρεσβεία prehz•_vee_•ah

emerald σμαράγδι zmah•_rahgh_•THee

emergency έκτακτη ανάγκη _ehk_•tahk•tee ah•_nah_•gee

emergency exit έξοδος κινδύνου _eh_•ksoh•THohs keen•_THee_•noo

empty adj άδειος ahTH•yohs

end n τέλος _teh_•lohs; v τελειώνω teh•lee•_oh_•noh

engine μηχανή mee•khah•_nee_

England Αγγλία ahng•_lee_•ah

English adj αγγλικός ahng•lee•_kohs_; (nationality) Άγγλος _ahng_•lohs; (language) αγγλικά ahng•lee•_kah_

enjoy ευχαριστιέμαι ehf•khah•rees•_tieh_•meh

enough αρκετά ahr•keh•_tah_

entertainment guide οδηγός ψυχαγωγίας oh•THee•_ghohs_ psee•khah•ghoh•_yee_•ahs

entrance fee τιμή εισόδου tee•_mee_ ee•_soh_•THoo

epileptic επιληπτικός eh•pee•leep•tee•_kohs_

error λάθος _lah_•thohs

escalator κυλιόμενες σκάλες kee•lee•_oh_•meh•nehs skah•lehs

essential απαραίτητος ah•pah•_reh_•tee•tohs

e-ticket ηλεκτρονικό εισιτήριο ee•lehk•troh•nee•_koh_ ee•see•_tee_•ree•oh

European Union Ευρωπαϊκή Ένωση ehv•roh•pah•ee•_kee_ eh•noh•see

euro ευρώ ehv•_roh_

evening βράδυ _vrah_•THee

examination (medical) ιατρική εξέταση ee•ah•tree•_kee_ eh•_kseh_•tah•see

example παράδειγμα pah•_rah_•THeegh•mah

excess baggage υπέρβαρο ee•_pehr_•vah•roh

exchange v (money) αλλάζω ah•_lah_•zoh

exchange rate τιμή συναλλάγματος tee•_mee_ see•nah•_lahgh_•mah•tohs

excursion εκδρομή ehk•THroh•_mee_

exhibition έκθεση _ehk_•theh•see

exit n έξοδος _eh_•ksoh•THohs

expensive ακριβός ahk•ree•_vohs_

expiration date ημερουμηνία λήξεως ee•meh•roh•_mee_•nee•ah lee•kseh•ohs

exposure (photos) στάση _stah_•see

express (mail) εξπρές ehk•_sprehs_

extension (number) εσωτερική γραμμή eh•soh•theh•ree•_kee_ ghrah•_mee_

extra (additional) άλλο ένα _ah_•loh eh•_nah_

eye n μάτι _mah_•tee

F

fabric (cloth) ύφασμα _ee_•fahs•mah

face n πρόσωπο _proh_•soh•poh

facial καθαρισμός προσώπου kah•thah•reez•_mohs_ proh•_soh_•poo

facility εξυπηρέτηση eh•kssee•pee•_reh_•tee•see

faint λιποθυμώ lee•poh•thee•_moh_

fall v πέφτω _pehf_•toh

family οικογένεια ee•koh•_yeh_•nee•ah

famous διάσημος _THee_•ah•see•mohs

fan n (air) ανεμιστήρας ah•neh•mees•_tee_•rahs

far adv μακριά mahk•ree•_ah_

fare εισιτήριο ee•see•_tee_•ree•oh

farm n φάρμα _fahr_•mah

fast adv γρήγορα _ghree_•ghoh•rah

fat adj (person) παχύς pah•_khees_

faucet βρύση _vree_•see

fault λάθος _lah_•thohs

favorite αγαπημένος ah•ghah•pee•_meh_•nohs

fax facility υπηρεσία φαξ ee•pee•reh•_see_•ah fahks

feed v ταΐζω tah•_ee_•zoh

female θηλυκός thee•lee•_kohs_

fence n φράχτης _frahkh_•tees

ferry φέρυ-μπωτ _feh_•ree•boht

festival φεστιβάλ fehs•tee•_vahl_

fever πυρετός pee•reh•_tohs_

fiancé αρραβωνιαστικός ah•rah•voh•niahs•tee•_kohs_

fiancée αρραβωνιαστικιά ah•rah•voh•niahs•tee•_kiah_

filling (dental) σφράγισμα _sfrah_•yeez•mah

film n (camera) φιλμ feelm

filter n φίλτρο _feel_•troh

fine adv καλά kah•_lah_; n πρόστιμο _prohs_•tee•moh

finger n δάχτυλο _THakh_•tee•loh

fire n φωτιά foh•_tiah_

fire brigade [BE] πυροσβεστική pee•rohz•vehs•tee•_kee_

fire escape έξοδος κινδύνου _eh_•ksoh•THohs keen•_THee_•noo

fire extinguisher πυροσβεστήρας pee•rohz•vehs•_tee_•rahs

first class πρώτη θέση _proh_•tee _theh_•see

first-aid kit κουτί πρώτων βοηθειών koo•_tee_ proh•tohn voh•ee•thee•_ohn_

fishing ψάρεμα _psah_•reh•mah

flag n σημαία see•_meh_•ah

flashlight φακός fah•_kohs_

flat adj επίπεδος eh•_pee_•peh•THohs; n διαμέρισμα THee•ah•_mehr_•eez•mah

flea ψύλλος _psee_•lohs

flight πτήση _ptee_•see

flight number αριθμός πτήσεως
ah•reeth•mohs ptee•seh•ohs
flip-flops σαγιονάρες
sah•yoh•nah•rehs
flood n πλημμύρα *plee•mee•rah*
florist ανθοπωλείο
ahn•thoh•poh•lee•oh
flower n λουλούδι *loo•loo•THee*
flu γρίπη *ghree•pee*
flush τραβώ το καζανάκι
trah•voh toh kah•zah•nah•kee
fly n μύγα *mee•ghah;* v πετάω
peh•tah•oh
follow v ακολουθώ
ah•koh•loo•thoh
foot πόδι *poh•THee*
football [BE] ποδόσφαιρο
poh•THOhs•feh•roh
footpath μονοπάτι
moh•noh•pah•tee
forecast n πρόβλεψη
prohv•leh•psee
foreign ξένος *kseh•nohs*
foreign currency ξένο
συνάλλαγμα *kseh•noh*
see•nah•lahgh•mah
forest n δάσος *THah•sohs*
forget ξεχνώ *ksehkh•noh*
form n έντυπο *ehn•dee•poh*
fortunately ευτυχώς
ehf•tee•khohs
forward προωθώ *proh•oh•thoh*
fountain συντριβάνι
seen•dree•vah•nee
free adj *(available)* ελεύθερος
eh•lehf•theh•rohs
freezer κατάψυξη
kah•tah•psee•ksee
frequent adj συχνός *seekh•nohs*
fresh adj φρέσκος *frehs•kohs*
friend n φίλος *fee•lohs*
frightened φοβισμένος
foh•veez•meh•nohs
from από *ah•poh*
front n προκυμαία
proh•kee•meh•ah

full adj γεμάτος *yeh•mah•tohs*
furniture έπιπλα *eh•peep•lah*
fuse n ασφάλεια *ahs•fah•lee•ah*

G

gambling τζόγος *joh•ghohs*
game (toy) παιχνίδι
pehkh•nee•THee
garage γκαράζ *gah•rahz*
garden n κήπος *kee•pohs*
gas βενζίνη *vehn•zee•nee*
gas station βενζινάδικο
vehn•zee•nah•THee•koh
gastritis γαστρίτιδα
ghahs•tree•tee•THah
gate (airport) έξοδος
eh•ksoh•THohs
genuine αυθεντικός
ahf•thehn•dee•kohs
get off (transport) κατεβαίνω
kah•teh•veh•noh
get out (of vehicle) βγαίνω
vyeh•noh
gift δώρο *THoh•roh*
gift store κατάστημα με είδη
δώρων *kah•tahs•tee•mah meh
ee•THee THoh•rohn*
girl κορίτσι *koh•ree•tsee*
girlfriend φίλη *fee•lee*
give δίνω *THee•noh*
glass (container) ποτήρι
poh•tee•ree
glasses (optical) γυαλιά
yah•liah
glove n γάντι *ghahn•dee*
go πηγαίνω *pee•yeh•noh*
gold v χρυσός *khree•sohs*
golf γκολφ *gohlf*
golf course γήπεδο γκολφ
yee•peh•THoh gohlf
good καλός *kah•lohs*
grass γρασίδι *ghrah•see•THee*
gratuity φιλοδώρημα
fee•loh•THoh•ree•mah
greasy (hair, skin) λιπαρός
lee•pah•rohs

Greece Ελλάδα *eh•lah•THah*
Greek adj ελληνικός
eh•lee•nee•kohs; (nationality) Έλληνας *eh•lee•nahs*
greengrocer [BE] οπωροπωλείο
oh•poh•roh•poh•lee•oh
ground (earth) έδαφος
eh•THah•fohs
group n γκρουπ *groop*
guarantee n εγγύηση
eh•gee•ee•see; v εγγυώμαι
eh•gee•oh•meh
guide book τουριστικός
οδηγός *too•ree•stee•kohs
oh•THee•ghohs*
guided tour ξενάγηση
kseh•nah•yee•see
guitar κιθάρα *kee•thah•rah*
gynecologist γυναικολόγος
yee•neh•koh•loh•ghohs

H

hair μαλλιά *mah•liah*
hairbrush βούρτσα *voor•tsah*
hair dresser κομμωτήριο
koh•moh•tee•ree•oh
hair dryer σεσουάρ
seh•soo•ahr
half μισός *mee•sohs*
hammer σφυρί *sfee•ree*
hand n χέρι *kheh•ree*
hand luggage αποσκευές χειρός
ah•pohs•keh•vehs khee•rohs
handbag τσάντα *tsahn•dah*
handicraft λαϊκή τέχνη
lah•ee•kee tehkh•nee
handicapped-accessible toilet
προσβάσιμη τουαλέτα για
ανάπηρους *prohs•vah•see•mee
too•ah•leh•tah yah
ah•nah•pee•roos*
handkerchief χαρτομάντηλο
khah•rtoh•mahn•dee•loh
handle n πόμολο *poh•moh•loh*
hanger κρεμάστρα
kreh•mahs•trah

harbor n λιμάνι lee•_mah_•nee

hat n καπέλο kah•_peh_•loh

have *(possession)* έχω eh•khoh

have to (obligation) οφείλω
oh•_fee_•loh

head n κεφάλι keh•_fah_•lee

headache πονοκέφαλος
poh•noh•_keh_•fah•lohs

health food store κατάστημα
με υγιεινές τροφές
kah•_tahs_•tee•mah meh
ee•yee•ee•_nehs_ troh•_fehs_

health insurance ασφάλεια
υγείας ahs•_fah_•lee•ah
ee•_yee_•ahs

hearing aid ακουστικό
βαρυκοΐας ah•koo•stee•_koh_
vah•ree•koh•_ee_•ahs

heart v καρδιά kahr•_THee_•ah

heart attack καρδιακό
έμφραγμα kahr•_THee_•ah•_koh_
ehm•frahgh•mah

heat wave καύσωνας
kahf•soh•nahs

heater (water) θερμοσίφωνας
thehr•moh•_see_•foh•nahs

heating θέρμανση
thehr•mahn•see

heavy βαρύς vah•_rees_

height ύψος ee•psohs

helicopter ελικόπτερο
eh•lee•_kohp_•teh•roh

help n βοήθεια voh•ee•thee•ah;
v βοηθώ voh•ee•_thoh_

here εδώ eh•_THoh_

highway εθνική οδός
ehth•nee•_kee_ oh•_THohs_

hike v κάνω πεζοπορία _kah_•noh
peh•zoh•poh•_ree_•ah

hill λόφος _loh_•fohs

hire [BE] v νοικιάζω nee•_kiah_•zoh

history ιστορία ee•stoh•_ree_•ah

hitchhiking οτοστόπ
oh•toh•_stohp_

hobby (pastime) χόμπυ
khoh•bee

hold on περιμένω
peh•ree•_meh_•noh

hole (in clothes) τρύπα _tree_•pah

holiday [BE] διακοπές
THee•ah•koh•_pehs_

honeymoon μήνας του μέλιτος
mee•nahs too meh•_lee_•tohs

horse track ιπποδρόμιο
ee•poh•_THroh_•mee•oh

hospital νοσοκομείο
noh•soh•koh•_mee_•oh

hot (weather) ζεστός zehs•_tohs_

hot spring θερμή πηγή
thehr•_mee_ pee•_yee_

hotel ξενοδοχείο
kseh•noh•THoh•_khee_•oh

household articles είδη
οικιακής χρήσεως ee•THee
ee•kee•ah•_kees_ khree•seh•ohs

husband σύζυγος _see_•zee•ghohs

|

ice n πάγος _pah_•ghohs

identification ταυτότητα
tahf•_toh_•tee•tah

illegal παράνομος
pah•_rah_•noh•mohs

illness αρρώστεια
ahr•_ohs_•tee•ah

imitation απομίμηση
ah•poh•_mee_•mee•see

immediately αμέσως
ah•_meh_•sohs

impressive εντυπωσιακός
ehn•dee•poh•see•ah•_kohs_

included συμπεριλαμβάνεται
seem•beh•ree•lahm•_vah_•
neh•teh

indigestion δυσπεψία
THehs•peh•_psee_•ah

indoor εσωτερικός
ee•soh•teh•ree•_kohs_

indoor pool εσωτερική
πισίνα ee•soh•teh•ree•_kee_
pee•_see_•nah

inexpensive φτηνός ftee•_nohs_

infected μολυσμένος
moh•leez•_meh_•nohs

inflammation φλεγμονή
flegh•moh•_nee_

information πληροφορίες
plee•roh•foh•_ree_•ehs

information office γραφείο
πληροφοριών ghrah•_fee_•oh
plee•roh•foh•ree•_ohn_

injection ένεση eh•neh•see

injured τραυματισμένος
trahv•mah•teez•_meh_•nohs

innocent αθώος ah•_thoh_•ohs

insect bite τσίμπημα από έντομο
tseem•bee•mah ah•_poh_
ehn•doh•mah

insect repellent
εντομοαπωθητικό ehn•doh•
moh•ah•poh•thee•tee•_koh_

inside μέσα _meh_•sah

insist επιμένω eh•pee•_meh_•noh

insomnia αϋπνία
ah•eep•_nee_•ah

instruction οδηγία
oh•THee•_yee_•ah

insulin ινσουλίνη
een•soo•_lee_•nee

insurance ασφάλεια
ahs•_fah_•lee•ah

insurance certificate
πιστοποιητικό ασφάλειας
pees•toh•pee•ee•tee•_koh_
ahs•_fah_•lee•ahs

insurance claim ασφάλεια
αποζημίωσης ahs•_fah_•lee•ah
ah•poh•zee•_mee_•oh•sees

**insurance com-
pany** ασφαλιστική εταιρία
ahs•fah•lees•tee•_kee_
eh•teh•_ree_•ah

interest rate επιτόκιο
eh•pee•_toh_•kee•oh

interesting ενδιαφέρων
ehn•THee•ah•_feh_•rohn

international διεθνής
THee•eth•_nees_

**International Student
Card** διεθνής φοιτητική
κάρτα THee•ehth•<u>nees</u>
fee•tee•tee•<u>kee</u> kahr•tah
internet ίντερνετ ee•nteh•rnet
internet cafe ίντερνετ καφέ
ee•nteh•rnet kah•<u>feh</u>
interpreter διερμηνέας
THee•ehr•mee•<u>neh</u>•ahs
interval διάλειμμα
THee•<u>ah</u>•lee•mah
introduce συστήνω see•<u>stee</u>•noh
introductions συστάσεις
see•<u>stah</u>•sees
invitation πρόσκληση
prohs•klee•see
invite v προσκαλώ prohs•kah•<u>loh</u>
iodine ιώδειο ee•oh•THee•oh
iron n σίδερο <u>see</u>•THeh•roh; v
σιδερώνω see•THeh•<u>roh</u>•noh
itemized bill αναλυτικός
λογαριασμός ah•nah•lee•tee•
kohs loh•ghahr•yahz•mohs

J

jacket σακάκι sah•<u>kah</u>•kee
jammed σφηνωμένος
sfee•noh•<u>meh</u>•nohs
jar n βάζο vah•zoh
jaw σαγόνι sah•<u>ghoh</u>•nee
jeans μπλου-τζην bloo•jeen
jellyfish μέδουσα meh•THoo•sah
jet-ski τζετ-σκι jeht•skee
jeweler κοσμηματοπωλείο kohz•
mee•mah•toh•poh•<u>lee</u>•oh
job δουλειά THoo•liah
jogging τζόγκινγκ joh•geeng
joke n ανέκδοτο
ah•<u>nehk</u>•THoh•toh
journey ταξίδι tah•<u>ksee</u>•THee
junction (intersection) κόμβος
kohm•vohs

K

keep v κρατώ krah•<u>toh</u>
key n κλειδί klee•<u>THee</u>

key card κάρτα-κλειδί
<u>kahr</u>•tah•klee•<u>dee</u>
key ring μπρελόκ breh•<u>lohk</u>
kidney νεφρό nehf•<u>roh</u>
kind n είδος ee•THohs
king βασιλιάς vah•see•<u>liahs</u>
kiosk περίπτερο
peh•<u>ree</u>•pteh•roh
kiss n φιλί fee•<u>lee</u>; v φιλώ
fee•<u>loh</u>
kitchen χαρτί κουζίνας khah•<u>rtee</u>
koo•<u>zee</u>•nahs
knapsack σάκκος sah•kohs
knee γόνατο <u>ghoh</u>•nah•toh
knife μαχαίρι mah•<u>kheh</u>•ree
know γνωρίζω ghnoh•<u>ree</u>•zoh

L

label n ετικέτα eh•tee•<u>keh</u>•tah
ladder σκάλα skah•lah
lake λίμνη <u>leem</u>•nee
lamp λάμπα <u>lahm</u>•bah
land n γη ghee; v προσγειώνομαι
prohz•yee•<u>oh</u>•noh•meh
language course μάθημα ξένης
γλώσσας <u>mah</u>•thee•mah
<u>kseh</u>•nees ghloh•sahs
large adj μεγάλος meh•<u>ghah</u>•lohs
last τελευταίος teh•lehf•<u>teh</u>•ohs
late adv αργά ahr•<u>ghah</u>
laugh v γελώ yeh•<u>loh</u>
laundry facility πλυντήριο
pleen•<u>dee</u>•ree•oh
lavatory μπάνιο <u>bah</u>•nioh
lawyer δικηγόρος
THee•kee•<u>ghoh</u>•rohs
laxative καθαρτικό
kah•thahr•tee•<u>koh</u>
learn μαθαίνω mah•<u>theh</u>•noh
leave v (depart) φεύγω <u>fehv</u>•ghoh;
(let go) αφήνω ah•<u>fee</u>•noh
left adj αριστερός
ah•rees•teh•<u>rohs</u>; adv
αριστερά ah•rees•teh•<u>rah</u>
leg πόδι <u>poh</u>•THee
legal νόμιμος <u>noh</u>•mee•mohs

lend δανείζω THah•<u>nee</u>•zoh
length μήκος <u>mee</u>•kohs
lens φακός fah•<u>kohs</u>
lens cap κάλυμμα φακού
<u>kah</u>•lee•mah fah•<u>koo</u>
less λιγότερο lee•<u>ghoh</u>•teh•roh
letter γράμμα <u>ghrah</u>•mah
level (even) επίπεδο
eh•<u>pee</u>•peh•THoh
library βιβλιοθήκη
veev•lee•oh•<u>thee</u>•kee
lie down ξαπλώνω ksah•<u>ploh</u>•noh
life boat ναυαγοσωστική λέμβος
nah•vah•ghoh•sohs•tee•<u>kee</u>
<u>lehm</u>•vohs
lifeguard ναυαγοσώστης
nah•vah•ghoh•<u>sohs</u>•tees
life jacket σωσίβιο
soh•<u>see</u>•vee•oh
lift [BE] n (elevator) ασανσέρ
ah•sahn•<u>sehr</u>
lift pass άδεια σκι <u>ah</u>•THee•ah
skee
light adj (color) ανοιχτός
ah•neekh•<u>tohs</u>; n (electric)
φως fohs
light bulb λάμπα <u>lahm</u>•bah
lighter adj ανοιχτότερος
ah•neekh•<u>toh</u>•teh•rohs; n
αναπτήρας ah•nahp•<u>tee</u>•rahs
lighthouse φάρος <u>fah</u>•rohs
lights (car) φώτα <u>foh</u>•tah
line n (subway) γραμμή
ghrah•<u>mee</u>
lips χείλη <u>khee</u>•lee
lipstick κραγιόν krah•<u>yohn</u>
liter λίτρο <u>lee</u>•troh
little μικρός meek•<u>rohs</u>
liver συκώτι see•<u>koh</u>•tee
living room σαλόνι sah•<u>loh</u>•nee
local τοπικός toh•pee•<u>kohs</u>
location (space) θέση theh•see
lock n (door) κλειδαριά
klee•THah•<u>ryah</u>; (river,
canal) φράγμα <u>frahgh</u>•mah; v
κλειδώνω klee•<u>THoh</u>•noh

long adj μακρύς mak•_rees_

long-distance bus υπεραστικό λεωφορείο ee•peh•rahs•tee•_koh_ leh•oh•foh•_ree_•oh

long-distance call υπεραστικό τηλεφώνημα ee•pehr•ahs•tee•_koh_ tee•leh•_foh_•nee•mah

long-sighted [BE] πρεσβύωπας prehz•_vee_•oh•pahs

look v κοιτώ kee•_tah_•oh

look for ψάχνω psahkh•noh

loose (fitting) φαρδύς fahr•_THees_

loss n απώλεια ah•_poh_•lee•ah

lotion λοσιόν loh•_siohn_

loud adj δυνατός THee•nah•_tohs_

love v αγαπώ ah•ghah•_poh_

lower adj (berth) κάτω _kah_•toh

lubricant λιπαντικό lee•pahn•dee•_koh_

luck τύχη _tee_•khee

luggage αποσκευές ah•pohs•keh•_vehs_

luggage cart καροτσάκι αποσκευών kah•roh•_tsah_•kee ah•pohs•keh•_vohn_

luggage locker θυρίδα thee•_ree_•THah

lukewarm χλιαρός khlee•ah•_rohs_

lump n σβώλος _svoh_•lohs; (medical) εξόγκωμα eh•_ksoh_•goh•mah

lunch n μεσημεριανό meh•see•mehr•yah•_noh_

lung πνεύμονας _pnehv_•moh•nahs

luxury πολυτέλεια poh•lee•_teh_•lee•ah

M

magazine περιοδικό peh•ree•oh•THee•_koh_

magnificent μεγαλοπρεπής meh•ghah•lohp•reh•_pees_

mailbox ταχυδρομικό κουτί tah•

kheeTH•roh•mee•_koh_ koo•tee

mail n αλληλογραφία ah•lee•lohgh•rah•_fee_•ah

main κύριος _kee_•ree•ohs

make-up μακιγιάζ mah•kee•_yahz_

man (male) άνδρας _ahn_•THrahs

manager διευθυντής THee•ehf•theen•_dees_

manicure μανικιούρ mah•nee•_kioor_

manual (car) χειροκίνητος khee•roh•_kee_•nee•tohs

map n χάρτης _khahr_•tees

market n αγορά ah•ghoh•_rah_

married παντρεμένος pahn•dreh•_meh_•nohs

mask n (diving) μάσκα _mahs_•kah

mass n (church) λειτουργία lee•toor•_yee_•ah

massage n μασάζ mah•_sahz_

match n (sport) αγώνας ah•_ghoh_•nahs; (fire starter) σπίρτο speer•_toh_

maybe ίσως ee•_sohs_

meal γεύμα _yehv_•mah

mean v σημαίνω see•_meh_•noh

measure v μετρώ meht•_roh_

measurement μέτρηση _meh_•tree•see

medication φάρμακα _fahr_•mah•kah

meet συναντώ see•nahn•_doh_

memorial μνημείο mnee•_mee_•oh

mend διορθώνω THee•ohr•_thoh_•noh

menstrual cramp πόνος περιόδου poh•nohs peh•ree•oh•_THoo_

mention αναφέρω ah•nah•_feh_•roh

message n μήνυμα _mee_•nee•mah

metal n μέταλλο meh•_tah_•loh

microwave (oven) φούρνος μικροκυμάτων _foor_•nohs mee•kroh•kee•_mah_•tohn

migraine ημικρανία ee•mee•krah•_nee_•ah

mileage χιλιόμετρα khee•_lioh_•meh•trah

mini-bar μινι-μπαρ _mee_•nee•bahr

minimart παντοπωλείο pahn•doh•poh•_lee_•oh

minimum ελάχιστος eh•_lah_•khees•tohs

minute n (time) λεπτό lehp•_toh_

mirror n καθρέφτης kah•_threhf_•tees

mistake λάθος _lah_•thohs

misunderstanding παρεξήγηση pah•reh•_ksee_•yee•see

mobile phone [BE] κινητό kee•nee•_toh_

modern μοντέρνος moh•_dehr_•nohs

moisturizer (cream) ενυδατική κρέμα eh•nee•THah•tee•_kee_ _kreh_•mah

money χρήματα _khree_•mah•tah

money order ταχυδρομική επιταγή tah•kheeTH•roh•mee•_kee_ eh•pee•tah•_yee_

money-belt ζώνη για χρήματα _zoh_•nee yah _khree_•mah•tah

monument μνημείο mnee•_mee_•oh

moped μοτοποδήλατο moh•toh•poh•_THee_•lah•toh

more παραπάνω pah•rah•_pah_•noh

morning πρωί proh•_ee_

mosquito κουνούπι koo•_noo_•pee

mosquito bite τσίμπημα κουνουπιού _tseem_•bee•mah koo•noo•_piooh_

motorboat εξωλέμβιο eh•ksoh•_lehm_•vee•oh

motorway [BE] εθνική οδός ehth•nee•_kee_ oh•_THohs_

mountain βουνό voo•_noh_

moustache μουστάκι
moos•_tah_•kee

mouth n στόμα _stoh_•mah

move v *(room)* μετακομίζω
meh•tah•koh•_mee_•zoh

movie ταινία teh•_nee_•ah

movie theater κινηματογράφος
kee•nee•mah•tohgh•_rah_•fohs

much πολύ poh•_lee_

muscle n μυς mees

museum μουσείο moo•_see_•oh

music μουσική moo•see•_kee_

musician μουσικός
moo•see•kohs

must v πρέπει _preh_•pee

N

nail salon σαλόνι νυχιών
sah•_loh_•nee nee•_khiohn_

name n όνομα _oh_•noh•mah

napkin πετσέτα peh•_tseh_•tah

nappy [BE] πάνα μωρού _pah_•nah
moh•_roo_

narrow στενός steh•_nohs_

national εθνικός eth•nee•_kohs_

nationality υπηκοότητα
ee•pee•koh•_oh_•tee•tah

nature φύση _fee_•see

nature reserve εθνικός δρυμός
eth•nee•_kohs_ THree•_mohs_

nature trail μονοπάτι
moh•noh•_pah_•tee

nausea ναυτία nahf•_tee_•ah

near adv κοντά kohn•_dah_

nearby εδώ κοντά eh•_THoh_
kohn•_dah_

necessary απαραίτητος
ah•pah•_reh_•tee•tohs

necklace κολλιέ koh•_lieh_

need v χρειάζομαι
khree•_ah_•zoh•meh

neighbor n γείτονας
yee•toh•nahs

nerve νεύρο _nehv_•roh

never ποτέ poh•_teh_

new καινούργιος keh•_noor_•yohs

newspaper εφημερίδα
eh•fee•meh•_ree_•THah

newsstand περίπτερο
peh•_ree_•pteh•roh

next επόμενος eh•_poh_•meh•nohs

next to δίπλα THeep•lah

night νύχτα _neekh_•tah

night club νυχτερινό κέντρο
neekh•teh•ree•_noh_ kehn•droh

noisy θορυβώδης
thoh•ree•_voh_•THees

none adj κανένας kah•_neh_•nahs

non-smoking μη καπνίζοντες
mee kap•_nee_•zohn•dehs

north βόρεια _voh_•ree•ah

nose n μύτη _mee_•tee

nudist beach παραλία
γυμνιστών pah•rah•_lee_•ah
yeem•nees•_tohn_

nurse n νοσοκόμα
noh•soh•_koh_•mah

O

occupied κατειλημένος
kah•tee•lee•_meh_•nohs

office γραφείο ghrah•_fee_•oh

old adj *(thing)* παλιός pah•_liohs_;
(person) γέρικος _yeh_•ree•kohs

old town παλιά πόλη pah•_liah_
poh•lee

old-fashioned ντεμοντέ
deh•mohn•_deh_

once μια φορά miah foh•_rah_

one-way ticket απλό εισιτήριο
ahp•_loh_ ee•see•_tee_•ree•oh

open adj ανοιχτός ah•neekh•_tohs_;
v ανοίγω ah•_nee_•ghoh

opening hours ώρες λειτουργίας
_oh_•rehs lee•toor•_yee_•ahs

opera όπερα oh•_peh_•rah

opposite απέναντι
ah•_peh_•nahn•dee

optician οφθαλμίατρος
ohf•thahl•_mee_•aht•rohs

orchestra ορχήστρα
ohr•_khees_•trah

order v παραγγέλνω
pah•rah•_gehl_•noh

organized οργανωμένος
ohr•ghah•noh•_meh_•nohs

others άλλα _ah_•lah

out adv έξω _eh_•ksoh

outdoor εξωτερικός
eh•ksoh•teh•ree•_kohs_

outside adj έξω _eh_•ksoh

oval οβάλ oh•_vahl_

oven φούρνος _foor_•nohs

over there εκεί eh•_kee_

overnight (package) ένα βράδυ
_eh_•nah vrah•THee

owe χρωστώ khroh•_stoh_

owner κάτοχος kah•toh•khohs

P

pacifier πιπίλα pee•_pee_•lah

pack v *(baggage)* φτιάχνω τις
βαλίτσες ftee•_ahkh_•noh tees
vah•_lee_•tsehs

paddling pool [BE] ρηχή πισίνα
ree•_khee_ pee•_see_•nah

padlock λουκέτο loo•_keh_•toh

pain n πόνος poh•nohs

painkiller παυσίπονο
pahf•_see_•poh•noh

paint v ζωγραφίζω
zohgh•rah•_fee_•zoh

pair ζευγάρι zehv•_ghah_•ree

pajamas πυτζάμες pee•_jah_•mehs

palace ανάκτορα
ah•_nahk_•toh•rah

panorama πανόραμα
pah•_noh_•rah•mah

pants παντελόνι
pahn•deh•_loh_•nee

paper χαρτί khar•_tee_

paralysis παράλυση
pah•rah•lee•_see_•ah

parcel πακέτο pah•_keh_•toh

parents γονείς ghoh•_nees_

park n πάρκο _pahr_•koh

parking lot χώρος στάθμευσης
khoh•rohs _stahth_•mehf•sees

parking meter παρκόμετρο
pahr•<u>koh</u>•meht•roh

party *n* (social gathering) πάρτυ
<u>pah</u>•tee

pass *v* περνώ *pehr•<u>noh</u>*

passenger επιβάτης
eh•pee•<u>vah</u>•tees

passport διαβατήριο
THiah•vah•<u>tee</u>•ree•oh

pastry store ζαχαροπλαστείο
zah•khah•rohp•lahs•<u>tee</u>•oh

path μονοπάτι *moh•noh•<u>pah</u>•tee*

pay *v* πληρώνω *plee•<u>roh</u>•noh*

payment πληρωμή *plee•roh•<u>mee</u>*

peak *n* κορυφή *koh•ree•<u>fee</u>*

pearl μαργαριτάρι
mahr•ghah•ree•<u>tah</u>•ree

pebbly (beach) με χαλίκια *meh
khah•<u>lee</u>•kiah*

pedestrian crossing διάβαση
πεζών *THee•<u>ah</u>•vah•see
peh•<u>zohn</u>*

pedestrian zone πεζόδρομος
peh•<u>zohTH</u>•roh•mohs

pen *n* στυλό *stee•<u>loh</u>*

per την *teen*

perhaps ίσως *ee•sohs*

period (menstrual) περίοδος
peh•<u>ree</u>•oh•THohs; (time)
χρονική περίοδος *khroh•
nee•<u>kee</u> peh•<u>ree</u>•oh•THos*

permit *n* άδεια *<u>ah</u>•THee•ah*

petrol [BE] βενζίνη
vehn•<u>zee</u>•nee

pewter κασσίτερος
kah•<u>see</u>•teh•rohs

phone *n* τηλέφωνο
tee•<u>leh</u>•foh•noh

phone call τηλεφώνημα
tee•leh•<u>foh</u>•nee•mah

phone card τηλεκάρτα
tee•leh•<u>kahr</u>•tah

photo *v* φωτογραφία
foh•tohgh•rah•<u>fee</u>•ah

photocopier φωτοτυπικό
foh•toh•tee•pee•<u>koh</u>

phrase *n* φράση *<u>frah</u>•see*

pick up παίρνω *pehr•<u>noh</u>*

picnic area περιοχή για
πικνίκ *peh•ree•oh•<u>khee</u> yah
peek•<u>neek</u>*

piece τεμάχιο *teh•<u>mah</u>•khee•oh*

pillow μαξιλάρι
mah•ksee•<u>lah</u>•ree

pillow case μαξιλαροθήκη
mah•ksee•lah•roh•<u>thee</u>•kee

pipe (smoking) πίπα *<u>pee</u>•pah*

piste [BE] μονοπάτι
moh•noh•<u>pah</u>•tee

pizzeria πιτσαρία
pee•tsah•<u>ree</u>•ah

plan *n* σχέδιο *<u>skheh</u>•THee•oh*

plane *n* αεροπλάνο
ah•eh•rohp•<u>lah</u>•noh

plant *n* φυτό *fee•<u>toh</u>*

plastic wrap διαφανή
μεμβράνη *THee•ah•fah•<u>nee</u>
mehm•<u>vrah</u>•nee*

platform αποβάθρα
ah•poh•<u>vahth</u>•rah

platinum πλατίνα *plah•<u>tee</u>•nah*

play *v* (games) παίζω *peh•<u>zoh</u>;
(music) παίζω *peh•<u>zoh</u>*

playground παιδική χαρά
peh•THee•<u>kee</u> khah•<u>rah</u>

pleasant ευχάριστος
ehf•<u>khah</u>•rees•tohs

plug *n* πρίζα *<u>pree</u>•zah*

point *n* σημείο *see•<u>mee</u>•oh; *v*
δείχνω *<u>THeekh</u>•noh*

poison *n* δηλητήριο
THee•lee•<u>tee</u>•ree•oh

poisonous δηλητηριώδης
THee•lee•tee•ree•<u>oh</u>•THees

police *n* αστυνομία
ah•stee•noh•<u>mee</u>•ah

police station αστυνομικό
τμήμα *ah•stee•noh•mee•<u>koh</u>
<u>tmee</u>•mah*

pond *n* λιμνούλα *leem•<u>noo</u>•lah*

popular δημοφιλής
THee•moh•fee•<u>lees</u>

porter αχθοφόρος
ahkh•thoh•<u>foh</u>•rohs

portion *n* μερίδα *meh•<u>ree</u>•THah*

possible πιθανός *pee•thah•<u>nohs</u>*

postbox [BE] ταχυδρομικό κουτί
*tah•khee TH•roh•mee•<u>koh</u>
koo•<u>tee</u>*

post card καρτποστάλ
kahrt•poh•<u>stahl</u>

post office ταχυδρομείο
tah•khee THroh•<u>mee</u>•oh

pottery αγγειοπλαστική
ahn•gee•ohp•lahs•tee•<u>kee</u>

pound (sterling) λίρα *<u>lee</u>•rah*

pregnant έγκυος *<u>eh</u>•gee•ohs*

prescribe συνταγογραφώ
seen•dah•ghoh•ghrah•<u>foh</u>

prescription συνταγή γιατρού
seen•dah•<u>yee</u> yaht•<u>roo</u>

present δώρο *THoh•roh*

press *v* σιδερώνω
see•THeh•<u>roh</u>•noh

pretty δι όμορφος
<u>oh</u>•mohr•fohs

prison *n* φυλακή *fee•lah•<u>kee</u>*

private bathroom ιδιωτικό
μπάνιο *ee•THee•oh•tee•<u>koh</u>
<u>bah</u>•nioh*

problem πρόβλημα
prohv•lee•mah

program *n* πρόγραμμα
prohgh•rah•mah

program of events πρόγραμμα
θεαμάτων *<u>prohgh</u>•rah•mah
theh•ah•<u>mah</u>•tohn*

prohibited απαγορευμένος
ah•pah•ghoh•rehv•<u>meh</u>•nohs

pronounce προφέρω
proh•<u>feh</u>•roh

public δημόσιος
THee•<u>moh</u>•see•ohs

public holiday αργία
ahr•<u>yee</u>•ah

pump *n* τρόμπα *troh•mbah*

purpose σκοπός *skoh•<u>pohs</u>*

put *v* βάζω *vah•<u>zoh</u>*

Q

quality ποιότητα pee•_oh_•tee•tah

quantity ποσότητα poh•_soh_•tee•tah

quarantine n καραντίνα kah•rahn•_dee_•nah

quarter (quantity) ένα τέταρτο _eh_•nah teh•tah•rtoh

quay αποβάθρα ah•poh•_vath_•rah

question n ερώτηση eh•_roh_•tee•see

queue [BE] v περιμένω στην ουρά peh•ree•_meh_•noh steen oo•_rah_

quick γρήγορος _ghree_•ghoh•rohs

quiet adj ήσυχος ee•see•khohs

R

racket (tennis, squash) ρακέτα rah•_keh_•tah

radio n ραδιόφωνο rah•_THee_•oh•foh•noh

railway station [BE] σιδηροδρομικός σταθμός see•_THee_•rohTH•roh•mee•kohs stahth•_mohs_

rain n βροχή vroh•_khee_; v βρέχει _vreh_•khee

raincoat αδιάβροχο ah•_THee_•ahv•roh•khoh

rapids ρεύμα ποταμού _rehv_•mah poh•tah•_moo_

rare (unusual) σπάνιος _spah_•nee•ohs

rash n εξάνθημα eh•_ksahn_•thee•mah

ravine ρεματιά reh•mah•_tiah_

razor ξυραφάκι ksee•rah•_fah_•kee

razor blade ξυραφάκι ksee•rah•_fah_•kee

ready adj έτοιμος eh•_tee_•mohs

real (genuine) γνήσιος _ghee_•see•ohs; **(true)** αληθινός ah•lee•thee•nohs

receipt απόδειξη ah•_poh_•THee•ksee

reception (hotel) ρεσεψιόν reh•seh•_psiohn_

recommend συστήνω sees•_tee_•noh

reduction έκπτωση _ehk_•ptoh•see

refund n επιστροφή χρημάτων eh•pees•troh•_fee_ khree•mah•tohn

region περιοχή peh•ree•oh•_khee_

registration number αριθμός κυκλοφορίας ah•reeth•_mohs_ kee•kloh•foh•_ree_•ahs

religion θρησκεία three•_skee_•ah

remember θυμάμαι thee•_mah_•meh

rent v νοικιάζω nee•_kiah_•zoh

repair n επισκευή eh•pee•skeh•_vee_; v επισκευάζω eh•pee•skeh•_vah_•zoh

repeat v επαναλαμβάνω eh•pah•nah•lahm•_vah_•noh

replacement part ανταλλακτικό ahn•dah•lahk•tee•_koh_

report v αναφέρω ah•nah•_feh_•roh

restaurant εστιατόριο ehs•tee•ah•_toh_•ree•oh

restroom τουαλέτα too•ah•_leh_•tah

retired συνταξιούχος seen•dah•ksee•_oo_•khohs

return ticket [BE] εισιτήριο με επιστροφή ee•see•_tee_•ree•oh meh eh•pee•stroh•_fee_

reverse the charges με χρέωση του καλούμενου meh _khreh_•oh•see too kah•_loo_•meh•noo

revolting αηδιαστικός ah•ee•THee•ah•stee•_kohs_

rib πλευρό pleh•_vroh_

right adj **(correct)** σωστός soh•_stohs_; **(side)** δεξιός THeh•ksee•_ohs_

river ποταμός poh•tah•_mohs_

road δρόμος _THroh_•mohs

road assistance οδική βοήθεια oh•_THee_•kee voh•_ee_•thee•ah

road sign πινακίδα pee•nah•_kee_•Thah

robbery ληστεία lees•_tee_•ah

rock n βράχος _vrah_•khohs

rock climbing αναρρίχηση ah•_nah_•ree•khee•see

romantic ρομαντικός roh•mahn•dee•_kohs_

roof n στέγη _steh_•yee

room n δωμάτιο THoh•_mah_•tee•oh

room service υπηρεσία δωματίου ee•pee•reh•_see_•ah THoh•mah•_tee_•oo

rope n σχοινί skhee•_nee_

round adj στρογγυλός strohn•gkee•_lohs_; n **(of golf)** παιχνίδι peh•kh•_nee_•THee

round-trip ticket εισιτήριο με επιστροφή ee•see•_tee_•ree•oh meh eh•pee•stroh•_fee_

route n διαδρομή THee•ahTH•roh•_mee_

rowing κωπηλασία koh•pee•lah•_see_•ah

rubbish [BE] σκουπίδια skoo•_peeTH_•yah

rude αγενής ah•yeh•_nees_

rug χαλί khah•_lee_

run v τρέχω _treh_•khoh

rush hour ώρα αιχμής _oh_•rah ehkh•_mees_

S

safe adj **(not dangerous)** ασφαλής ahs•fah•_lees_

sailing boat ιστιοπλοϊκό ees•tee•oh•plo•ee•_koh_

sales tax ΦΠΑ fee•pee•_ah_

same ίδιος eeTHee•ohs

sand άμμος _ah_•mohs

sandals πέδιλα _peh_•THee•lah

sandy (beach) με άμμο meh _ah_•moh

sanitary napkin σερβιέτα
sehr•vee•<u>eh</u>•tah

satin σατέν sah•<u>tehn</u>

saucepan κατσαρόλα
kah•tsah•<u>roh</u>•lah

sauna σάουνα <u>sah</u>•oo•nah

scarf κασκόλ kahs•<u>kohl</u>

scissors ψαλίδι psah•<u>lee</u>•THee

scratch γρατζουνιά
ghrah•joo•<u>niah</u>

screw n βίδα vee•<u>THah</u>

screwdriver κατσαβίδι
kah•tsah•<u>vee</u>•THee

sea θάλασσα <u>thah</u>•lah•sah

seafront προκυμαία
proh•kee•<u>meh</u>•ah

seat n θέση <u>theh</u>•see

second-hand shop κατάστημα
μεταχειρισμένων ειδών kah•
<u>tah</u>•stee•mah meh•tah•
khee•reez•<u>meh</u>•nohn ee•<u>THohn</u>

sedative ηρεμιστικό
ee•reh•mee•stee•<u>koh</u>

see βλέπω vleh•poh

send στέλνω stehl•noh

senior citizen ηλικιωμένος
ee•lee•kee•oh•<u>meh</u>•nohs

separately ξεχωριστά
kseh•khoh•ree•<u>stah</u>

service n (business) υπηρεσία
ee•pee•reh•<u>see</u>•ah; (mass)
λειτουργία lee•toor•<u>yee</u>•ah

service charge χρέωση
υπηρεσίας <u>khreh</u>•oh•see
ee•pee•reh•<u>see</u>•ahs

sewer υπόνομος
ee•<u>poh</u>•noh•mohs

shade (color) απόχρωση
ah•<u>pohkh</u>•roh•see; (darkness) σκιά skee•<u>ah</u>

shampoo n σαμπουάν
sahm•poo•<u>ahn</u>

shape n σχήμα <u>skhee</u>•mah

shaving cream κρέμα
ξυρίσματος <u>kreh</u>•mah
ksee•<u>reez</u>•mah•tohs

shelf n ράφι <u>rah</u>•fee

ship n πλοίο <u>plee</u>•oh

shirt πουκάμισο
poo•<u>kah</u>•mee•soh

shock (electric)
ηλεκτροπληξία
ee•leh•ktroh•plee•<u>ksee</u>•ah

shoe παπούτσι pah•<u>poo</u>•tsee

shoe polish βερνίκι
παπουτσιών vehr•<u>nee</u>•kee
pah•poo•<u>tsiohn</u>

shoe repair επισκευή
παπουτσιών eh•pee•skeh•<u>vee</u>
pah•poo•<u>tsiohn</u>

shoe store κατάστημα
υποδημάτων
kah•<u>tah</u>•stee•mah
ee•poh•<u>THee</u>•<u>mah</u>•tohn

shop (store) κατάστημα
kah•<u>tah</u>•stee•mah

shopping mall εμπορικό κέντρο
ehm•boh•ree•<u>koh</u> <u>keh</u>•ntroh

shore n ακτή ahk•<u>tee</u>

short adj κοντός kohn•<u>dohs</u>

shorts n σορτς sohrts

short-sighted [BE] μύωπας
<u>mee</u>•oh•pahs

shoulder n (anatomy) ώμος
<u>oh</u>•mohs

show δείχνω <u>THeekh</u>•noh

shower n ντους dooz

shower gel αφρόλουτρο για
ντους ahf•<u>roh</u>•loot•roh
yah dooz

shut adj κλειστός klees•<u>tohs</u>

sick adj άρρωστος <u>ah</u>•rohs•tohs

side (of road) μεριά mehr•<u>yah</u>

sightseeing sight αξιοθέατο
ah•ksee•oh•<u>theh</u>•ah•toh

sightseeing tour ξενάγηση στα
αξιοθέατα kseh•<u>nah</u>•yee•see
stah ah•ksee•oh•<u>theh</u>•ah•tah

sign (road) σήμα <u>see</u>•mah

silk μετάξι meh•<u>tah</u>•ksee

silver ασήμι ah•<u>see</u>•mee

simple απλός ahp•<u>lohs</u>

single (not married) ελεύθερος
eh•<u>lehf</u>•theh•rohs

single room μονόκλινο
δωμάτιο moh•<u>noh</u>•klee•noh
THoh•<u>mah</u>•tee•oh

single ticket [BE] απλό
εισιτήριο ahp•<u>loh</u>
ee•see•<u>tee</u>•ree•oh

sink (bathroom) νιπτήρας
nee•<u>ptee</u>•rahs

sit κάθομαι <u>kah</u>•thoh•meh

size n μέγεθος <u>meh</u>•yeh•thohs

skates παγοπέδιλα
pah•ghoh•<u>peh</u>•THee•lah

skating rink παγοδρόμιο
pah•ghohTH•<u>roh</u>•mee•oh

ski boots μπότες του σκι
<u>boh</u>•tehs too skee

ski poles μπαστούνια του σκι
bahs•<u>too</u>•niah too skee

ski school σχολή σκι skhoh•<u>lee</u>
skee

skiing σκι skee

skin n δέρμα <u>Thehr</u>•mah

skirt φούστα <u>foo</u>•stah

sleep v κοιμάμαι kee•<u>mah</u>•meh

sleeping bag υπνόσακκος
ee•<u>pnoh</u>•sah•kohs

sleeping car βαγκόν-λι
vah•<u>gohn</u>•lee

sleeping pill υπνωτικό χάπι
eep•noh•tee•<u>koh</u> <u>khah</u>•pee

slippers παντόφλες
pahn•<u>dohf</u>•lehs

slope (ski) πλαγιά plah•<u>yah</u>

slow adj αργός ahr•<u>ghohs</u>

small μικρός meek•<u>rohs</u>

smell v μυρίζω mee•<u>ree</u>•zoh

smoke v καπνίζω kahp•<u>nee</u>•zoh

smoking area περιοχή για
καπνίζοντες peh•ree•oh•<u>khee</u>
yah kahp•nee•<u>zohn</u>•dehs

snack bar κυλικείο
kee•lee•<u>kee</u>•oh

sneakers αθλητικά παπούτσια
ath•lee•tee•<u>kah</u> pah•<u>poo</u>•tsiah

snorkeling equipment εξοπλισμό για ελεύθερη κατάδυση eh•ksohp•leez•moh yah eh•lehf•theh•ree kah•tah•THEE•see

snow v χιονίζει khioh•nee•zee

soap n σαπούνι sah•poo•nee

soccer ποδόσφαιρο poh•THOhs•feh•roh

socket πρίζα pree•zah

socks κάλτσες kahl•tsehs

sofa καναπές kah•nah•pehs

sole (shoes) σόλα soh•lah

something κάτι kah•tee

sometimes μερικές φορές meh•ree•kehs foh•rehs

soon σύντομα seen•doh•mah

soother [BE] πιπίλα pee•pee•lah

sore throat πονόλαιμος poh•noh•leh•mohs

sort n είδος ee•THOhs; v διαλέγω THiah•leh•ghoh

south adj νότιος noh•tee•ohs

souvenir σουβενίρ soo•veh•neer

souvenir store κατάστημα σουβενίρ kah•tahs•tee•mah soo•veh•neer

spa σπα spah

space n (area) χώρος khoh•rohs

spare (extra) επιπλέον eh•peep•leh•ohn

speak μιλώ mee•loh

special requirement ειδική ανάγκη ee•THee•kee ah•nahn•gkee

specialist ειδικός ee•THee•kohs

specimen δείγμα THeegh•mah

speed v τρέχω treh•khoh

spend ξοδεύω ksoh•THeh•voh

spine σπονδυλική στήλη spohn•THee•lee•kee stee•lee

spoon n κουτάλι koo•tah•lee

sport αθλητισμός ahth•lee•teez•mohs

sporting goods store κατάστημα αθλητικών ειδών kah•tahs•tee•mah ath•lee•tee•kohn ee•THOhn

sports massage αθλητικό μασάζ ahth•lee•tee•koh mah•sahz

sports stadium αθλητικό στάδιο ahth•lee•tee•koh stah•THee•oh

square τετράγωνος teht•rah•ghoh•nohs

stadium στάδιο stah•THee•oh

stain n λεκές leh•kehs

stairs σκάλες skah•lehs

stale μπαγιάτικος bah•yah•tee•kohs

stamp n (postage) γραμματόσημο ghrah•mah•toh•see•moh

start v αρχίζω ahr•khee•zoh

statement (legal) δήλωση THee•loh•see

statue άγαλμα ah•ghahl•mah

stay v μένω meh•noh

sterilizing solution αποστειρωτικό διάλυμα ah•pohs•tee•roh•tee•koh THee•ah•lee•mah

sting n (insect) τσίμπημα tsee•bee•mah

stolen κλεμένος kleh•meh•nohs

stomach n στομάχι stoh•mah•khee

stomachache στομαχόπονος stoh•mah•khoh•poh•nohs

stop n (bus) στάση stah•see; v σταματώ stah•mah•toh

store guide [BE] οδηγός καταστήματος oh•THee•ghohs kah•tahs•tee•mah•tohs

stove κουζίνα koo•zee•nah

straight ahead ευθεία ehf•thee•ah

strange παράξενος pah•rah•kseh•nohs

straw (drinking) καλαμάκι kah•lah•mah•kee

stream n ρυάκι ree•ah•kee

street δρόμος THroh•mohs

string n (cord) σπάγκος spah•gohs

student φοιτητής fee•tee•tees

study v σπουδάζω spoo•THah•zoh

style n στυλ steel

subtitled με υπότιτλους meh ee•poh•teet•loos

subway μετρό meh•troh

subway station σταθμός μετρό stahth•mohs meh•troh

suggest προτείνω proh•tee•noh

suit (men's) κουστούμι koos•too•mee; (women's) ταγιέρ tah•yehr

suitable κατάλληλος kah•tah•lee•lohs

sunburn n έγκαυμα ηλίου ehn•gahv•mah ee•lee•oo

sunglasses γυαλιά ηλίου yah•liah ee•lee•oo

sunshade [BE] ομπρέλλα ohm•breh•lah

sunstroke ηλίαση ee•lee•ah•see

sun tan lotion λοσιόν μαυρίσματος loh•siohn mahv•rees•mah•tohs

sunscreen αντιηλιακό ahn•dee•ee•lee•ah•koh

superb έξοχος eh•ksoh•khohs

supermarket σουπερμάρκετ soo•pehr•mahr•keht

supervision επίβλεψη eh•peev•leh•psee

surname επίθετο eh•pee•theh•toh

sweatshirt φούτερ foo•tehr

swelling πρήξιμο pree•ksee•moh

swimming κολύμβηση koh•leem•vee•see

swimming pool πισίνα pee•see•nah

swimming trunks μαγιό mah•yoh

swimsuit μαγιό mah•yoh

switch n διακόπτης
THiah•*koh*•ptees

swollen πρησμένος
preez•*meh*•nohs

symptom σύμπτωμα
seem•ptoh•mah

T

table τραπέζι trah•*peh*•zee

tablecloth τραπεζομάντηλο
trah•peh•zoh•*mahn*•dee•loh

tablet χάπι *khah*•pee

take παίρνω *pehr*•noh

take a photograph βγάζω
φωτογραφία *vghah*•zoh
foh•tohgh•rah•*fee*•ah

take away [BE] πακέτο για το
σπίτι pah•*keh*•toh yah toh
spee•tee

tall ψηλός psee•*lohs*

tampon ταμπόν tahm•*bohn*

tax n φόρος *foh*•rohs

taxi ταξί tah•*ksee*

taxi driver ταξιτζής
tah•ksee•*jees*

taxi rank [BE] πιάτσα ταξί
piah•tsah tah•*ksee*

teaspoon κουταλάκι
koo•tah•*lah*•kee

team n ομάδα oh•*mah*•THah

teenager έφηβος eh•fee•vohs

telephone n τηλέφωνο
tee•*leh*•foh•noh

telephone booth τηλεφωνικός
θάλαμος tee•leh•foh•nee•*kohs*
thah•lah•mohs

telephone call κλήση *klee*•see

telephone directory τηλεφωνικός
κατάλογος tee•leh•foh•
nee•*kohs* kah•*tah*•loh•ghohs

telephone number αριθμός
τηλεφώνου ah•reeth•*mohs*
tee•leh•*foh*•noo

tell λέω *leh*•oh

temperature (body) θερμοκρασία
theh•rmohk•rah•*see*•ah

temple ναός nah•*ohs*

temporary προσωρινός
proh•soh•ree•*nohs*

tennis τέννις *teh*•nees

tennis court γήπεδο τέννις
yee•peh•THoh *teh*•nees

tent σκηνή skee•*nee*

terrible φοβερός foh•veh•*rohs*

theater θέατρο *theh*•aht•roh

theft κλοπή kloh•*pee*

there εκεί eh•*kee*

thermal bath ιαματικό λουτρό
ee•ah•mah•tee•*koh* loot•*roh*

thermos flask θερμός thehr•*mohs*

thick χοντρός khohn•*drohs*

thief κλέφτης *klehf*•tees

thin adj λεπτός lehp•*tohs*

think νομίζω noh•*mee*•zoh

thirsty διψάω THee•*psah*•oh

those εκείνα eh•*kee*•nah

throat λαιμός leh•*mohs*

thumb αντίχειρας
ahn•*dee*•khee•rahs

ticket εισιτήριο
ee•see•*tee*•ree•oh

ticket office γραφείο
εισιτηρίων ghrah•*fee*•oh
ee•see•tee•*ree*•ohn

tie n γραβάτα ghrah•*vah*•tah

tight adj στενός steh•*nohs*

tights [BE] η καλσόν kahl•*sohn*

timetable [BE] δρομολόγιο
THroh•moh•*loh*•yee•oh

tire λάστιχο *lahs*•tee•khoh

tired κουρασμένος
koo•rahz•*meh*•nohs

tissue χαρτομάντηλο
khahr•toh•*mahn*•dee•loh

toaster τοστιέρα toh•*stieh*•rah

tobacco καπνός kahp•*nohs*

tobacconist καπνοπωλείο
kahp•noh•poh•*lee*•oh

toilet [BE] τουαλέτα
too•ah•*leh*•tah

toilet paper χαρτί υγείας
khahr•*tee* ee•*yee*•ahs

toiletries καλλυντικά
kah•leen•dee•*kah*

tongue γλώσσα *ghloh*•sah

too (extreme) πάρα πολύ
pah•rah poh•*lee*

tooth δόντι *THohn*•dee

toothache πονόδοντος
poh•*noh*•THohn•dohs

toothbrush οδοντόβουρτσα
oh•*THohn*•*doh*•voor•tsah

toothpaste οδοντόπαστα
oh•*THohn*•*doh*•pahs•tah

top adj πάνω *pah*•noh

torn σχισμένος skheez•*meh*•nohs

tour guide ξεναγός
kseh•nah•*ghohs*

tourist τουρίστας too•*rees*•tahs

towards προς prohs

tower πύργος *peer*•ghohs

town πόλη *poh*•lee

town hall δημαρχείο
THee•mahr•*khee*•oh

toy store κατάστημα
παιχνιδιών kah•*tahs*•tee•mah
peh•khnee•*THiohn*

traditional παραδοσιακός
pah•rah•THoh•see•ah•*kohs*

traffic κίνηση *kee*•nee•see

trail μονοπάτι moh•noh•*pah*•tee

trailer τροχόσπιτο
troh•*khohs*•pee•toh

train τρένο *treh*•noh

train station σταθμός των
τρένων stahth•*mohs* tohn
treh•nohn

tram τραμ trahm

transfer μεταφέρω
meh•tah•*feh*•roh

transit n μεταφορά
meh•tah•foh•*rah*

translate μεταφράζω
meh•tah•*frah*•zoh

translation μετάφραση
meh•*tah*•frah•see

translator μεταφραστής
meh•tah•frah•*stees*

trash σκουπίδια *skoo•peeTH•yah*

trash can κάδος απορριμμάτων *kah•THohs ah•poh•ree•mah•tohn*

travel agency ταξιδιωτικό γραφείο *tah•ksee•THyoh•tee•koh ghrah•fee•oh*

travel sickness [BE] ναυτία *nahf•tee•ah*

traveler's check ταξιδιωτική επιταγή *tah•ksee•THee•oh•tee•kee tah•pah•yee*

tray δίσκος *THees•kohs*

tree δέντρο *THehn•droh*

trim n διόρθωμα *THee•ohr•thoh•mah*

trolley [BE] **(cart)** καροτσάκι *kah•roh•tsah•kee*

trolley-bus τρόλλεϋ *troh•leh•ee*

trousers [BE] παντελόνι *pahn•deh•loh•nee*

try on δοκιμάζω *THoh•kee•mah•zoh*

T-shirt μπλουζάκι *bloo•zah•kee*

tunnel τούνελ *too•nehl*

turn v γυρίζω *yee•ree•zoh*

turn down v *(volume, heat)* χαμηλώνω *khah•mee•loh•noh*

turn off v σβήνω *svee•noh*

turn on v ανάβω *ah•nah•voh*

turn up v *(volume, heat)* ανεβάζω *ah•neh•vah•zoh*

TV τηλεόραση *tee•leh•oh•rah•see*

twin bed διπλό κρεβάτι *THeep•loh kreh•vah•tee*

typical τυπικός *tee•pee•kohs*

U

ugly άσχημος *ahs•khee•mohs*

unconscious αναίσθητος *ah•nehs•thee•tohs*

underground [BE] υπόγειος *ee•poh•ghee•ohs*

underpants [BE] κυλοτάκι *kee•loh•tah•kee*

understand καταλαβαίνω *kah•tah•lah•veh•noh*

uneven (ground) ανώμαλος *ah•noh•mah•lohs*

unfortunately δυστυχώς *THees•tee•khohs*

uniform n στολή *stoh•lee*

unique μοναδικός *moh•nah•THee•kohs* unit μονάδα *moh•nah•THah*

United Kingdom Ηνωμένο Βασίλειο *ee•noh•meh•noh vah•see•lee•oh*

United States Ηνωμένες Πολιτείες *ee•noh•meh•nehs poh•lee•tee•es*

university Πανεπιστήμιο *pah•neh•pees•tee•mee•oh*

unlimited mileage απεριόριστα χιλιόμετρα *ah•peh•ree•ohr•ees•tah khee•lioh•meht•rah*

unpleasant δυσάρεστος *THee•sah•reh•stohs*

upper (berth) πάνω (κουκέτα) *pah•noh (koo•keh•tah)*

upstairs επάνω *eh•pah•noh*

urgent επείγον *eh•pee•ghohn*

use v χρησιμοποιώ *khree•see•moh•pee•oh*

useful χρήσιμος *khree•see•mohs*

V

vacancy ελεύθερο δωμάτιο *eh•lehf•theh•roh THoh•mah•tee•oh*

vacant ελεύθερος *eh•lehf•theh•rohs*

vacation διακοπές *THee•ah•koh•pehs*

vacation resort θέρετρο διακοπών *theh•reh•troh THee•ah•koh•pohn*

vaccination εμβόλιο *ehm•voh•lee•oh*

valid ισχύει *ee•skhee•ee*

valley κοιλάδα *kee•lah•THah*

valuable πολύτιμος *poh•lee•tee•mohs*

value n αξία *ah•ksee•ah*

VAT [BE] ΦΠΑ *fee•pee•ah*

vegetarian χορτοφάγος *khohr•toh•fah•ghohs*

vein φλέβα *fleh•vah*

velvet βελούδο *veh•loo•THoh*

very πολύ *poh•lee*

video βιντεοκασέτα *vee•deh•oh•kah•seh•tah*

video game παιχνίδι βίντεο *pehkh•nee•THee vee•deh•oh*

village χωριό *khohr•yoh*

visa βίζα *vee•zah*

visit n επίσκεψη *eh•pees•keh•psee*

volleyball βόλεϋ *voh•leh•ee*

vomit v κάνω εμετό *kah•noh eh•meh•toh*

W

wait v περιμένω *peh•ree•meh•noh*

waiter n γκαρσόν *gahr•sohn*

waitress δεσποινίς *THehs•pee•nees*

wake v ξυπνώ *kseep•noh*

walk v περπατώ *pehr•pah•toh*

walking route διαδρομή περιήγησης *THee•ah•THroh•mee peh•ree•ee•yee•sees*

wall τοίχος *tee•khohs*

wallet πορτοφόλι *pohr•toh•foh•lee*

want θέλω *theh•loh*

warm ζεστός *zehs•tohs*

washing machine πλυντήριο *pleen•dee•ree•oh*

watch n ρολόι *roh•loh•ee*

watch strap λουρί ρολογιού *loo•ree roh•loh•yioo*

water n νερό *neh•roh*

waterfall καταρράχτης *kah•tah•rahkh•tees*

waterproof αδιάβροχος
ah•*THee*•*ahv*•roh•khohs
wave n κύμα *kee*•mah
way δρόμος *THroh*•mohs
wear v φορώ foh•*roh*
weather καιρός keh•*rohs*
weather forecast πρόβλεψη
καιρού *prohv*•leh•psee keh•*roo*
wedding γάμος *ghah*•mohs
west δυτικά THee•tee•*kah*
wetsuit στολή δύτη stoh•*lee*
THee•tee
wheelchair αναπηρική
καρέκλα ah•nah•pee•ree•*kee*
kah•*rehk*•lah
wide φαρδύς fahr•*THees*
wife σύζυγος *see*•zee•ghohs
window παράθυρο
pah•*rah*•thee•roh

window seat θέση δίπλα στο
παράθυρο *theh*•see *THeep*•lah
stoh pah•*rah*•thee•roh
winery οινοποιείο
ee•noh•pee•*ee*•oh
wireless internet ασύρματο
ίντερνετ ah•*see*•rmah•toh
ee•nteh•rnet
with με meh
withdraw κάνω ανάληψη
kah•noh ah•*nah*•lee•psee
without χωρίς khoh•*rees*
witness μάρτυρας *mahr*•tee•rahs
wood (forest) δάσος *THah*•sohs;
(material) ξύλο *ksee*•loh
work δουλειώ *THoo*•*leh*•voh
worry ανησυχώ ah•nee•see•*khoh*
worse χειρότερος
khee•*roh*•teh•rohs

wound (cut) πληγή plee•*yee*
write (down) γράφω *ghrah*•foh
wrong λάθος *lah*•thohs

X

x-ray ακτινογραφία
ahk•tee•nohgh•rah•*fee*•ah

Y

yacht γιωτ yoht
yellow κίτρινος *keet*•ree•nohs
young νέος *neh*•ohs
youth hostel ξενώνας
νεότητας kseh•*noh*•nahs
neh•*oh*•tee•tahs

Z

zoo ζωολογικός κήπος
zoh•oh•loh•yee•*kohs* kee•pohs

GREEK–ENGLISH

A

ATM ehee•tee•*ehm* ATM
άγαλμα ah•ghahl•mah statue
αγαπημένος ah•ghah•pee•
meh•nohs favorite
αγαπώ ah•ghah•*poh* v love
αγγειοπλαστική ahn•gee•ohp•
lahs•tee•*kee* pottery
Αγγλία ahng•*lee*•ah England
αγγλικά ahng•lee•*kah* English
language
αγγλικός ahng•lee•*kohs* adj
English
Άγγλος *ahng*•lohs English
(nationality)
αγενής ah•yeh•*nees* rude
αγορά ah•ghoh•*rah* n market
αγοράζω ah•ghoh•*rah*•zoh buy
αγόρι ah•*ghoh*•ree boy
αγώνας ah•*ghoh*•nahs n match
(sport)

άδεια ah•*THee*•ah n permit
άδεια σκι ah•*THee*•ah skee
lift pass
άδειος *ahTH*•yohs adj empty
αδιάβροχο ah•*THee*•
ahv•roh•khoh raincoat
αδιάβροχος ah•*THee*•*ahv*•
roh•khohs waterproof
αδύναμος ah•*THee*•nah•mohs
weak
αεροδρόμιο ah•eh•roh•
THroh•mee•oh airport
αεροπλάνο ah•eh•rohp•*lah*•noh
n plane
αεροπορική εταιρία
ah•eh•roh•poh•ree•*kee*
eh•teh•*ree*•ah airline
αεροπορικώς ah•eh•roh•
poh•ree•*kohs* airmail
αηδιαστικός ah•ee•*THee*•ah•
stee•*kohs* revolting

αθλητικά παπούτσια ath•lee•
tee•*kah* pah•*poo*•tsiah
sneakers
αθλητικό στάδιο ahth•lee•
tee•*koh stah*•THee•oh sports
stadium
αθλητικός όμιλος
ahth•lee•tee•*kohs*
oh•mee•lohs sports club
αθλητισμός ahth•lee•teez•*mohs*
sport
αθώος ah•*thoh*•ohs innocent
αιμορραγία eh•moh•rah•*yee*•ah
n bleed
αιμορραγώ eh•moh•rah•*yoh*
v bleed
αίθουσα συναυλιών
eh•thoo•sah see•nahv•lee•*ohn*
concert hall
ακολουθώ ah•koh•loo•*thoh*
v follow

ακουστικό βαρυκοΐας ah•koo•
stee•<u>koh</u> vah•ree•koh•<u>ee</u>•ahs
hearing aid

ακριβός ahk•ree•<u>vohs</u> expensive

ακτή ahk•<u>tee</u> n shore

ακτινογραφία ahk•tee•
nohgh•rah•<u>fee</u>•ah x-ray

ακυρώνω ah•kee•<u>roh</u>•noh
v cancel

αληθινός ah•lee•thee•<u>nohs</u> real
(genuine)

αλλά ah•<u>lah</u> conj but

άλλα ah•lah others

αλλαγή ah•lah•<u>yee</u> n change

αλλάζω ah•<u>lah</u>•zoh v exchange
(money)

αλλεργικός ahl•ehr•yee•<u>kohs</u>
allergic

αλληλογραφία ah•lee•lohgh•
rah•<u>fee</u>•ah n mail

άλλο ένα ah•loh <u>eh</u>•nah extra
(additional)

άλλος ah•lohs another

αλουμινόχαρτο ah•loo•mee•
<u>noh</u>•khah•rtoh aluminum foil

Αμερικανός ah•meh•ree•
kah•<u>nohs</u> n American

αμέσως ah•<u>meh</u>•sohs immediately

άμμος <u>ah</u>•mohs sand

ανάβω ah•<u>nah</u>•voh v turn on

αναίσθητος ah•<u>nehs</u>•thee•tohs
unconscious

ανάκτορα ah•<u>nahk</u>•toh•rah
palace

αναλυτικός λογαριασμός
ah•nah•lee•tee•<u>kohs</u> loh•
ghahr•yahz•<u>mohs</u> itemized bill

αναπηρική καρέκλα
ah•nah•pee•ree•<u>kee</u>
kah•<u>rehk</u>•lah wheelchair

αναπνευστήρας ah•nahp•
nehf•<u>stee</u>•rahs snorkel

αναπνέω ah•nahp•<u>neh</u>•oh breathe

αναπτήρας ah•nahp•<u>tee</u>•rahs n
lighter (cigarette)

αναρρίχηση ah•nah•<u>ree</u>•
khee•see rock climbing

ανατολικά ah•nah•toh•lee•<u>kah</u>
east

αναφέρω ah•nah•<u>feh</u>•roh
mention (report)

αναχώρηση ah•nah•<u>khoh</u>•
ree•see departure (travel)

άνδρας <u>ahn</u>•THrahs n male
(man)

ανεμιστήρας ah•neh•mees•
<u>tee</u>•rahs n fan (air)

ανεβάζω ah•neh•<u>vah</u>•zoh v turn
up (volume, heat)

ανέκδοτο ah•<u>nehk</u>•THoh•toh
n joke

ανησυχώ ah•nee•see•<u>khoh</u>
worry

ανθοπωλείο ahn•thoh•poh•
<u>lee</u>•oh florist

ανοίγω ah•<u>nee</u>•ghoh v open

ανοιχτήρι ah•neekh•<u>tee</u>•ree
can opener

ανοιχτός ah•neekh•<u>tohs</u> adj light
(color), open

ανοιχτότερος
ah•neekh•<u>toh</u>•teh•rohs adj
lighter (color)

ανταλλακτικό ahn•dah•
lahk•tee•<u>koh</u> replacement part

αντιβιοτικό ahn•dee•
vee•oh•tee•<u>koh</u> antibiotic

αντιηλιακό ahn•dee•ee•
lee•ah•<u>koh</u> sunscreen

αντισηπτική κρέμα
ahn•dee•seep•tee•<u>kee</u>
<u>kreh</u>•mah antiseptic cream

αντίχειρας ahn•<u>dee</u>•khee•rahs
thumb

ανώμαλος ah•<u>noh</u>•mah•lohs
uneven (ground)

αξεσουάρ ah•kseh•soo•<u>ahr</u>
accessory

αξία ah•<u>ksee</u>•ah n value

αξιοθέατο ah•ksee•oh•
<u>theh</u>•ah•tah sightseeing sight

απαγορευμένος ah•pah•ghoh•
rehv•<u>meh</u>•nohs prohibited

απαραίτητος ah•pah•<u>reh</u>•
tee•tohs essential, necessary

απασχολημένος ah•pahs•
khoh•lee•<u>meh</u>•nohs adj busy
(occupied)

απέναντι ah•<u>peh</u>•nahn•dee
opposite

απεριόριστα χιλιόμετρα
ah•peh•ree•<u>ohr</u>•ees•tah khee•
<u>lioh</u>•meht•rah unlimited mileage

απλό εισιτήριο ahp•<u>loh</u>
ee•see•<u>tee</u>•ree•oh one-way
[single BE] ticket

απλός ahp•<u>lohs</u> simple

από ah•<u>poh</u> from

απομίμηση ah•poh•<u>mee</u>•
mee•see imitation

αποβάθρα ah•poh•<u>vahth</u>•rah
platform, quay

απόγευμα ah•<u>poh</u>•yehv•mah
afternoon

απόδειξη ah•<u>poh</u>•THee•ksee
receipt

απορρυπαντικό ah•poh•
ree•pahn•dee•<u>koh</u> detergent

αποσμητικό ah•pohz•
mee•tee•<u>koh</u> deodorant

αποσκευές ah•pohs•keh•<u>vehs</u>
baggage [BE]

αποσκευές χειρός ah•pohs•
keh•<u>vehs</u> khee•<u>rohs</u> hand
luggage

αποστειρωτικό διάλυμα
ah•pohs•tee•roh•tee•<u>koh</u> THee•
<u>ah</u>•lee•mah sterilizing solution

απόχρωση ah•<u>pohkh</u>•rn•see
shade (color)

απώλεια ah•<u>poh</u>•lee•ah n loss

αργά ahr•<u>ghah</u> adv late

αργία ahr•<u>yee</u>•ah public holiday

αργός ahr•<u>ghohs</u> adj slow

αριθμός κυκλοφορίας
ah•reeth•<u>mohs</u> kee•kloh•
foh•<u>ree</u>•ahs registration number

αριθμός πτήσεως
ah•reeth•mohs ptee•seh•ohs
flight number

αριθμός τηλεφώνου *ah•reeth•mohs tee•leh•foh•noo*
telephone number

αριστερός *ah•rees•teh•rohs*
left *(adj)*

αριστερά *ah•rees•teh•rah*
left *(adv)*

αρκετά *ahr•keh•tah* enough

αρραβωνιαστικά *ah•rah•voh•niahs•tee•kiah* fiancée

αρραβωνιαστικός *ah•rah•voh•niahs•tee•kohs* fiancé

αρρώστεια *ah•rohs•tee•ah*
illness

άρρωστος *ah•rohs•tohs adj* sick

αρτοποιείο *ahr•toh•pee•ee•oh*
bakery

αρχάριος *ahr•khah•ree•ohs*
beginner

αρχίζω *v ahr•khee•zoh* start

ασανσέρ *ah•sahn•sehr n* lift
(elevator)

ασήμι *ah•see•mee* silver

ασύρματο ίντερνετ *ah•see•rmah•toh ee•nteh•rnet* wireless
internet

ασθενοφόρο *ahs•theh•noh•foh•roh* ambulance

ασθματικός *ahsth•mah•tee•kohs* asthmatic

ασπιρίνη *ahs•pee•ree•nee* aspirin

αστυνομία *ah•stee•noh•mee•ah n* police

αστυνομικό τμήμα
ah•stee•noh•mee•koh tmee•mah police station

ασφάλεια *ahs•fah•lee•ah n*
fuse; insurance

ασφάλεια αποζημίωσης
ahs•fah•lee•ah ah•poh•zee•mee•oh•sees insurance claim

ασφάλεια υγείας *ahs•fah•lee•ah ee•yee•ahs* health insurance

ασφαλής *ahs•fah•lees adj* safe
(not dangerous)

ασφαλιστική εταιρία *ahs•fah•lees•tee•kee eh•teh•ree•ah* insurance company

άσχημος *ahs•khee•mohs* ugly

άτομο με ειδικές ανάγκες
ah•toh•moh meh eh•THee•kehs ah•nahn•gehs disabled

ατύχημα *ah•tee•khee•mah*
accident

αυθεντικός *ahf•thehn•dee•kohs* genuine

αυθεντικότητα *ahf•thehn•dee•koh•tee•tah* authenticity

αϋπνία *ah•eep•nee•ah* insomnia

αυτοκίνητο
ahf•toh•kee•nee•toh car

αυχένας *ahf•kheh•nahs* neck
(part of body)

αφήνω *ah•fee•noh v* leave (let go)

αφορολόγητα είδη
ah•foh•roh•loh•yee•tah ee•THee duty-free goods

αφρόλουτρο για ντους *ahf•roh•loot•roh yah dooz* shower gel

αχθοφόρος *ahkh•thoh•foh•rohs* porter

Β

βαμβάκι *vahm•vah•kee* cotton

βαγκόν-λι *vah•gohn•lee*
sleeping car

βάζο *vah•zoh n* jar

βάζω *vah•zoh v* put

βαλές *vah•lehs* jack

βαρετός *vah•reh•tohs* boring

βάρκα *vahr•kah* boat

βαρύς *vah•rees* heavy

βασιλιάς *vah•see•liahs* king

βγαίνω *vyeh•noh* get out (of
vehicle)

βελούδο *veh•loo•THoh* velvet

βενζινάδικο
vehn•zee•nah•THee•koh gas
[petrol BE] station

βενζίνη *vehn•zee•nee* gasoline
[petrol BE]

βερνίκι παπουτσιών *vehr•nee•kee pah•poo•tsiohn* shoe polish

βήχας *vee•khahs n* cough

βήχω *vee•khoh v* cough

βιβλίο *veev•lee•oh n* book

βιβλιοθήκη
veev•lee•oh•thee•kee library

βιβλιοπωλείο *veev•lee•oh•poh•lee•oh* bookstore

βίδα *vee•THah n* screw

βίζα *vee•zah* visa

βιντεοκασέτα *vee•deh•oh•kah•seh•tah* video

βλάβη *vlah•vee* breakdown n (car)

βλέπω *vleh•poh* see

βοήθεια *voh•ee•thee•ah n* help

βοηθώ *voh•ee•thoh v* help

βόλεϊ *voh•leh•ee* volleyball

βόρεια *voh•ree•ah* north

βοτανικός κήπος
voh•tah•nee•kohs kee•pohs botanical garden

βουνό *voo•noh* mountain

βουρτσίζω *voor•tsee•zoh v* brush

βραδινό *vrah•THee•noh* dinner

βράδυ *vrah•THee* evening

βράζω *vrah•zoh* boil

βράχος *vrah•khohs n* rock

βρετανικός *vreh•tah•nee•kohs*
British adj

Βρετανός *vreh•tah•nohs* British
(nationality)

βρέχει *vreh•khee v* rain

βροχή *vroh•khee n* rain

βρύση *vree•see* faucet

βρώμικος *vroh•mee•kohs adj* dirty

Γ

γάμος *ghah•mohs* wedding

γάζα *ghah•zah* bandage

γαλάκτωμα για τα μαλλιά
ghah•lah•ktoh•mah yah tah mah•liah conditioner (hair)

γάντι *ghahn•dee n* glove

γαστρίτιδα ghahs•_tree_•tee•THah gastritis

γεμάτος yeh•_mah_•tohs adj full

γείτονας _yee_•toh•nahs n neighbor

γελώ yeh•_loh_ v laugh

γεμιστή yeh•mees•_tee_ stuffed olive

γέρικος _yeh_•ree•kohs old (person)

γεύμα _yehv_•mah meal

γέφυρα _yeh_•fee•rah n bridge (over water)

γη ghee n land

γήπεδο γκολφ _yee_•peh•THoh gohlf golf course

γήπεδο τέννις _yee_•peh•THoh teh•nees tennis court

γιατρός yah•_trohs_ doctor

γιωτ yoht yacht

γκαράζ gah•_rahz_ garage

γκαρσόν gahr•_sohn_ waiter

γκόλφ gohlf golf

γκρουπ groop n group

γλώσσα _ghloh_•sah tongue

γνωρίζω ghnoh•_ree_•zoh know

γόνατο _ghoh_•nah•toh knee

γονείς ghoh•_nees_ parents

γράμμα _ghrah_•mah letter

γραμματόσημο ghrah•mah•_toh_•see•moh n stamp (postage)

γραμμή ghrah•_mee_ n line (subway)

γραβάτα ghrah•_vah_•tah n tie

γρασίδι ghrah•_see_•THee grass

γραφείο ghrah•_fee_•oh office

γραφείο ανταλλαγής συναλλάγματος ghrah•_fee_•oh ahn•dah•lah•_yees_ see•nah•_lahgh_•mah•tohs currency exchange office

γραφείο εισιτηρίων ghrah•_fee_•oh ee•see•tee•_ree_•ohn ticket office

γραφείο πληροφοριών ghrah•_fee_•oh plee•roh•foh•ree•_ohn_ information office

γράφω _ghrah_•foh write (down)

γρήγορα _ghree_•ghoh•rah adv fast

γρήγορος _ghree_•ghoh•rohs quick

γρίππη _ghree_•pee flu

γυαλιά yah•_liah_ glasses (optical)

γυαλιά ηλίου yah•_liah_ ee•_lee_•oo sun glasses

γυναικολόγος yee•neh•koh•_loh_•ghohs gynecologist

γυρίζω yee•_ree_•zoh v turn

γωνία ghoh•_nee_•ah corner

Δ

δανείζω THah•_nee_•zoh lend

δάσος _THah_•sohs n forest (wood)

δάχτυλο _THakh_•tee•loh n finger

δείγμα _THeegh_•mah specimen

δείχνω _THeekh_•noh v point (show)

δέντρο _THehn_•droh tree

δεξιός THeh•_ksee_•ohs adj right (not left)

δέρμα _THehr_•mah n skin

δημαρχείο THee•mahr•_khee_•oh town hall

δημοφιλής THee•moh•fee•_lees_ popular

δηλητήριο THee•lee•_tee_•ree•oh n poison

δηλητηριώδης THee•lee•tee•ree•_oh_•THees poisonous

δηλώνω THee•_loh_•noh declare

δήλωση THee•_loh_•see statement (legal)

δημόσιος THee•_moh_•see•ohs public

διαμάντι THiah•_mahn_•dee n diamond

διαμέρισμα THee•_ah_•meh•reez•mah apartment

διάβαση πεζών THee•_ah_•vah•see peh•_zohn_ pedestrian crossing

διαβατήριο THee•vah•_tee_•ree•oh passport

διαβητικός THee•ah•vee•tee•_kohs_ diabetic

διαδρομή THee•ahTH•_roh_•mee n route

διάδρομος THee•_ah_•THroh•mohs aisle seat

διαζευγμένος THee•ah•zehv•_ghmeh_•nohs divorced

διακοπές THee•ah•koh•_pehs_ vacation [holiday BE]

διακόπτης THiah•_koh_•ptees n switch

διαμέρισμα THee•ah•mehr•ees•_mah_ n flat

διάρροια THee•_ah_•ree•ah diarrhea

διάσημος THee•_ah_•see•mohs famous

διεθνής THee•eth•_nees_ international

διεθνής φοιτητική κάρτα THee•ehth•_nees_ fee•tee•_tee•kee_ _kahr_•tah International Student Card

διερμηνέας THee•ehr•mee•_neh_•ahs interpreter

διεύθυνση THee•_ehf_•theen•see n address

διευθυντής THee•ehf•theen•_dees_ manager

δικηγόρος THee•kee•_ghoh_•rohs lawyer

δίκλινο δωμάτιο _THeek_•lee•noh THoh•_mah_•tee•oh double room

δίνω _THee_•noh give

διόρθωμα THee•_ohr_•thoh•mah n trim

δίπλα _THeep_•lah next to

διπλό κρεβάτι THeep•_loh_ kreh•_vah_•tee twin bed

δίσκος _THees_•kohs tray

διψάω THee•_psah_•oh thirsty

δοκιμάζω THoh•kee•_mah_•zoh

try on
δολάριο THoh•_lah_•ree•oh dollar
δόντι THohn•dee tooth
δοσολογία
THoh•soh•loh•_yee_•ah dosage
δουλειά THoo•_liah_ job
δουλεύω THoo•_leh_•voh work
δρομολόγιο
THroh•moh•_loh_•yee•oh
time table
δρόμος THroh•mohs road,
street, way
δυνατός THee•nah•_tohs_ adj loud
δυσάρεστος THee•_sah_•reh stohs
unpleasant
δύσκολος THee•skoh•lohs
difficult
δυσπεψία THees•peh•_psee_•ah
indigestion
δυστυχώς THees•tee•_khohs_
unfortunately
δυτικά THee•tee•_kah_ west
δωμάτιο THoh•_mah_•tee•oh
n room
δώρο _THoh_•roh gift

E

ελιά eh•_liah_ olive
εμβόλιο ehm•_voh_•lee•oh
vaccination
εμπορικό κέντρο
ehm•boh•ree•_koh_ keh•ntroh
shopping mall [centre BE]
εγγύηση eh•_gee_•ee•see n
guarantee
εγγυώμαι eh•gee•oh•meh v
guarantee
έγκαυμα ηλίου ehn•gahv•mah
ee•_lee_•oo n sun burn
έγκυος eh•gee•ohs pregnant
έδαφος eh•THah•fohs ground
(earth)
εδώ eh•_THoh_ here
εδώ κοντά eh•_THoh_ kohn•dah
nearby
εθνική οδός ehth•nee•_kee_

oh•_THohs_ highway, motorway
εθνικός eth•nee•_kohs_ national
εθνικός δρυμός eth•nee•_kohs_
THree•_mohs_ nature reserve
είμαι _ee_•meh be
είμαι κουφός koo•_fohs_ deaf
είδη οικιακής χρήσεως
ee•THee•ee•kee•ah•_kees_
khree•_seh_•ohs household
articles
ειδική ανάγκη ee•THee•_kee_
ah•_nahn_•gkee special
requirement
ειδικός ee•THee•_kohs_ specialist
είδος _ee_•THohs kind (sort)
εισιτήριο ee•see•_tee_•ree•oh
fare (ticket)
εισιτήριο με επιστροφή
ee•see•_tee_•ree•oh meh
eh•pee•stroh•_fee_ roundtrip
[return BE] ticket
εκδρομή ehk•THroh•_mee_
excursion
εκεί eh•_kee_ there, over there
εκείνα eh•_kee_•nah those
έκθεση ehk•theh•see exhibition
έκπτωση ehk•ptoh•see
reduction
έκτακτη ανάγκη _ehk_•tahk•tee
ah•_nahn_•gee emergency
ελάχιστος eh•_lah_•khees•tohs
minimum
ελεύθερο δωμάτιο
eh•_lehf_•theh•roh
THoh•_mah_•tee•oh vacancy
ελεύθερος eh•_lehf_•theh•rohs adj
free, single, vacant
ελικόπτερο
eh•lee•_kohp_•teh•roh
helicopter
Ελλάδα eh•_lah_•THah Greece
Έλληνας _eh_•lee•nahs Greek
(nationality)
ελληνικός eh•lee•nee•_kohs_
adj Greek
ένα βράδυ _eh_•nah vrah•THee

overnight
ένα τέταρτο _eh_•nah
teh•_tah_•rtoh quarter (quantity)
ενδιαφέρων en•THee•_ah_•
feh•rohn interesting
ένεση eh•_neh_•see injection
ενήλικας eh•_nee_•lee•kahs adult
ενοχλώ eh•noh•_khloh_ disturb
έντομο _ehn_•doh•moh insect
εντομοαπωθητικό ehn•doh•
moh•ah•poh•thee•tee•_koh_
insect repellent
έντυπο _ehn_•dee•poh n form
εντυπωσιακός ehn•dee•
poh•see•ah•_kohs_ impressive
ενυδατική κρέμα eh•nee•
THah•tee•_kee_ kreh•mah
moisturizer (cream)
εξάνθημα eh•_ksahn_•thee•mah
n rash
εξαργυρώνω
eh•ksahr•ghee•_roh_•noh v cash
εξόγκωμα eh•_ksoh_•goh•mah n
lump (medical)
έξοδος _eh_•ksoh•THohs n gate
(airport); exit
έξοδος κινδύνου
_eh_•ksoh•THohs keen•_THee_•noo
emergency, fire exit
εξοχή eh•ksoh•_khee_ countryside
έξοχος eh•ksoh•khohs superb
εξπρές ehk•_sprehs_ express (mail)
εξυπηρέτηση eh•ksee•peh•
reh•tee•see facility
έξω _eh_•ksoh adv out
έξω eh•ksoh adj outside
εξωλέμβιο eh•ksoh•_lehm_•
vee•oh motorboat
εξωτερικός
eh•ksoh•teh•ree•_kohs_ outdoor
επαναλαμβάνω eh•pah•nah•
lahm•_vah_•noh v repeat
επάνω eh•_pah_•noh upstairs
επείγον eh•_pee_•ghohn urgent
επιμένω eh•pee•_meh_•noh insist
επιβάτης eh•pee•_vah_•tees

passenger
επιβεβαιώνω eh•pee•veh•veh•_oh_•noh confirm
επίβλεψη eh•_peev_•leh•psee supervision
επίθεση eh•pee•_theh_•seh n attack
επίθετο eh•_pee_•theh•toh surname
επικοινωνώ eh•pee•kee•noh•_noh_ v contact
επιληπτικός eh•pee•leep•tee•_kohs_ epileptic
επίπεδο eh•_pee_•peh•THoh level (even)
επίπεδο eh•_pee_•peh•THohs adj flat
έπιπλα _eh_•peep•lah furniture
επιπλέον eh•peep•_leh_•ohn spare (extra)
επισκευάζω eh•pee•skeh•_vah_•zoh v repair
επισκευή eh•pee•skeh•_vee_ n repair
επισκευή παπουτσιών eh•pee•skeh•vee pah•poo•_tsiohn_ shoe repair
επίσκεψη eh•_pees_•keh•psee n visit
επιστροφή χρημάτων eh•pees•troh•_fee_ khree•_mah_•tohn n refund
επιταγή eh•pee•tah•_yee_ n check [cheque BE] (bank)
επιτίθεμαι eh•pee•_tee_•theh•meh v attack
επιτόκιο eh•pee•_toh_•kee•oh interest rate
επόμενος eh•_poh_•meh•nohs next
έρχομαι _ehr_•khoh•meh come
ερώτηση eh•_roh_•tee•see n question
εστιατόριο ehs•tee•ah•_toh_•ree•oh n restaurant
εσωτερική γραμμή eh•soh•theh•ree•_kee_

ghrah•_mee_ extension (number)
εσωτερική πισίνα eh•soh•teh•ree•_kee_ pee•_see_•nah indoor pool
εσωτερικός eh•soh•teh•ree•_kohs_ indoor
ετικέτα eh•tee•_keh_•tah n label
έτοιμος _eh_•tee•mohs adj ready
ευθεία ehf•_thee_•ah straight ahead
εύκολος _ehf_•koh•lohs adj easy
ευρώ ehv•_roh_ euro
Ευρωπαϊκή Ένωση ehv•roh•pah•ee•_kee_ _eh_•noh•see European Union
ευτυχώς ehf•tee•_khohs_ fortunately
ευχαριστιέμαι ehf•khah•rees•_tieh_•meh enjoy
ευχάριστος ehf•_khah_•rees•tohs pleasant
εφημερίδα eh•fee•mehree•_THah_ newspaper
έφηβος _eh_•fee•vohs teenager
έχω _eh_•khoh have (possession)

Z

ζαχαροπλαστείο zah•khah•rohp•lahs•_tee_•oh pastry store
ζεστός zes•_tohs_ hot, warm (weather)
ζημιά zee•_miah_ n damage
ζητώ zee•_toh_ ask
ζωγραφίζω zohgh•rah•_fee_•zoh v paint
ζωγράφος zohgh•_rah_•fohs painter
ζώνη _zoh_•nee belt
ζώνη για χρήματα _zoh_•nee yah khree•_mah_•tah money-belt

H

ημερομηνία λήξεως ee•meh•roh•mee•_nee_•ah lee•_kseh_•ohs expiration date
ημερολόγιο ee•meh•roh•

loh•_yee_•oh calendar
ημικρανία ee•mee•krah•_nee_•ah migraine
ηλεκτρικός ee•lehk•tree•_kohs_ electric
ηλεκτρονικό εισιτήριο ee•lehk•troh•nee•_koh_ ee•see•_tee_•ree•oh e-ticket
ηλεκτρονικό ταχυδρομείο ee•lehk•troh•nee•_koh_ tah•hee•dro•_mee_•oh (ee•meh•eel) e-mail
ηλεκτροπληξία ee•lehk•troh• plee•_ksee_•ah shock (electric)
ηλίαση ee•_lee_•ah•see sun stroke
ηλικιωμένος ee•lee•kee•oh• meh•nohs senior citizen
Ηνωμένες Πολιτείες ee•noh• _meh_•nehs poh•lee•_tee_•ehs United States
Ηνωμένο Βασίλειο ee•noh• _meh_•noh vah•_see_•lee•oh United Kingdom
ηρεμιστικό ee•reh•mee• stee•_koh_ sedative
ήσυχος _ee_•see•khohs adj quiet

θ

θάλασσα _thah_•lah•sah sea
θέατρο _theh_•aht•roh theater
θέλω _theh_•loh want
θέρμανση _thehr_•mahn•see heating
θερμή πηγή thehr•_mee_ pee•_yee_ hot spring
θερμόμετρο thehr•_moh_• meht•roh thermometer
θερμοκρασία theh•rmohk• rah•_see_•ah temperature (body)
θερμός thehr•_mohs_ thermos flask
θέρετρο διακοπών _theh_•reh• troh THee•ah•koh•_pohn_ vacation resort
θέση _theh_•see n location (space), seat

θέση δίπλα στο παράθυρο _theh•see_ THeep•lah stoh pah•_rah•_thee•roh window seat

θηλυκός thee•lee•_kohs_ female

θορυβώδης thoh•ree•_voh•_THees noisy

θρησκεία three•_skee•_ah religion

θυμάμαι thee•_mah•_meh remember

θυρίδα thee•_ree•_THah luggage locker (lock-up)

Ι

ιατρική εξέταση ee•ah•tree•_kee_ eh•_kseh•_tah•see examination (medical)

ίδιος _ee•_THee•ohs same

ιδιωτικό μπάνιο ee•THee•oh•tee•_koh_ bah•nioh private bathroom

ιερέας ee•eh•_reh•_ahs priest

ινσουλίνη een•soo•_lee•_nee insulin

ίντερνετ _ee•_nteh•rnet internet

ίντερνετ καφέ _ee•_nteh•rnet kah•_feh_ internet cafe

ιπποδρομία ee•poh•THroh•_mee•_ah horse racing

ιστιοπλοϊκό ees•tee•oh•ploh•ee•_koh_ sailing boat

ιστορία ee•stoh•_ree•_ah history

ισχύει ee•_skhee•_ee valid

ίσως _ee•_sohs maybe, perhaps

ιώδειο ee•_oh•_THee•oh iodine

Κ

κάδος απορριμμάτων _kah•_THohs ah•poh•ree•_mah•_tohn trash can

καθαρισμός προσώπου kah•thah•reez•_mohs_ proh•_soh•_poo facial

καθαρός kah•thah•_rohs_ clean

καθαρτικό kah•thahr•tee•_koh_ laxative

καθεδρικός ναός kah•theh•THree•_kohs_ nah•_ohs_ cathedral

καθήκον kah•_thee•_kohn duty (obligation)

κάθομαι _kah•_thoh•meh sit

καθρέφτης kah•_threhf•_tees n mirror

καθυστέρηση kah•thee•_steh•_ree•see n delay

καθυστερώ kah•thee•steh•_roh_ v delay

καινούργιος keh•_noor•_yohs new

καιρός keh•_rohs_ weather

καλά kah•_lah_ adv fine (well)

καλαμάκι kah•lah•_mah•_kee straw (drinking)

καλάθι kah•_lah•_THee basket

καλός kah•_lohs_ good

καλσόν kahl•_sohn_ n tights

κάλτσες _kahl•_tsehs socks

κάλυμμα φακού _kah•_lee•mah fah•_koo_ lens cap

καλώ kah•_loh_ v call

κάμπινγκ _kah•_mpeeng camping

καναπές kah•nah•_pehs_ sofa

κανένας kah•_neh•_nahs adj none

κάνω ανάληψη _kah•_noh ah•_nah•_lee•psee withdraw

κάνω εμετό _kah•_noh eh•meh•toh v vomit

κάνω κράτηση _kah•_noh _krah•_tee•see v book

κάνω πεζοπορία _kah•_noh peh•zoh•poh•_ree•_ah v hike

καπέλο kah•_peh•_loh hat

καπνίζω kahp•_nee•_zoh v smoke

καπνοπωλείο kahp•noh•poh•_lee•_oh tobacconist

καπνός kahp•_nohs_ tobacco

καραντίνα kah•rahn•_dee•_nah n quarantine

καράφα kah•_rah•_fah carafe

καρδιά kahr•_THee•_ah v heart

καρδιακό έμφραγμα kahr•THee•ah•_koh_ ehm•frahgh•mah heart attack

καροτσάκι kah•roh•_tsah•_kee trolley (cart)

καροτσάκια αποσκευών kah•roh•_tsah•_kiah ah•pohs•keh•_vohn_ baggage [BE] carts (trolleys)

κάρτα-κλειδί _kahr•_tah klee•_dee_ key card

καρτποστάλ kahrt•poh•_stahl_ post card

κασκόλ kahs•_kohl_ scarf

κασσίτερος kah•_see•_teh•rohs pewter

κάστρο _kahs•_troh castle

καταδυτικός εξοπλισμός kah•tah•THee•tee•_kohs_ eh•ksoh•pleez•_mohs_ diving equipment

καταλαβαίνω kah•tah•lah•_veh•_noh understand

κατάλληλος kah•_tah•_lee•lohs suitable

καταρράχτης kah•tah•_rahkh•_tees waterfall

κατάστημα kah•_tah•_stee•mah shop (store)

κατάστημα με αντίκες kah•_tah•_stee•mah meh ahn•_tee•_kehs antiques store

κατάστημα με είδη δώρων kah•_tah•_stee•mah meh _ee•_THee THOH•rohn gift store

κατάστημα με υγιεινές τροφές kah•_tah•_stee•mah meh ee•yee•eh•_nehs_ troh•_fehs_ health food store

κατάστημα μεταχειρισμένων ειδών kah•_tah•_stee•mah meh•tah•khee•reez•_meh•_nohn ee•_THohn_ second-hand shop

κατάστημα αθλητικών ειδών kah•_tah•_stee•mah ath•lee•tee•_kohn_ ee•_THohn_ sporting goods store

κατάστημα ρούχων kah•_tahs•_tee•mah _roo•_khohn clothing store

κατάστημα σουβενίρ
kah•tahs•tee•mah
soo•veh•neer souvenir store
κατάστημα υποδημάτων
kah•tah•stee•mah
ee•poh•THee•
mah•tohn shoe store
καταστρέφω kah•tah•streh•foh
v damage
κατάψυξη kah•tah•psee•ksee
freezer
κατεβαίνω kah•teh•veh•noh get
off (transport)
κατειλημένος kah•tee•
lee•meh•nohs occupied
κάτι kah•tee something
κάτοχος kah•toh•khohs owner
κατσαβίδι kah•tsah•vee•THee
screwdriver
κατσαρόλα kah•tsah•roh•lah
saucepan
κάτω kah•toh adj lower (berth)
καύσωνας kahf•soh•nahs
heat wave
καφετέρια kah•feh•teh•ree•ah
cafe
κέντρο της πόλης kehn•droh
tees poh•lees downtown area
κεφάλι keh•fah•lee n head
κήπος kee•pohs n garden
κιθάρα kee•thah•rah guitar
κινηματογράφος kee•nee•
mah•tohgh•rah•fohs movie
theater
κίνηση kee•nee•see traffic
κινητό kee•nee•toh cell phone
[mobile phone BE]
κίτρινος keet•ree•nohs yellow
κλειδαριά klee•THahr•yah n
lock (door)
κλειδί klee•THee n key
κλειδώνω klee•THoh•noh v
lock (door)
κλειστός klees•tohs adj shut
κλεμένος kleh•meh•nos stolen
κλέφτης klehf•tees thief

κλήση klee•see n call
κλιματισμός klee•mah•
teez•mohs air conditioning
κλοπή kloh•pee theft
κομμωτήριο koh•moh•
tee•ree•oh hair dresser
κόμβος kohm•vohs junction
(intersection)
κοιμάμαι kee•mah•meh v sleep
κοιλάδα kee•lah•THah valley
κοιτάω kee•tah•oh v look
κολύμβηση koh•leem•vee•see
swimming
κοντά kohn•dah adv near
κοντός kohn•dohs adj short
κορίτσι koh•ree•tsee girl
κορυφή koh•ree•fee n peak
κοσμηματοπωλείο kohz•mee•
mah•toh•poh•lee•oh jeweler
κουβέρτα koo•veh•rtah blanket
κουζίνα koo•zee•nah stove
κουνούπι koo•noo•pee mosquito
κουρασμένος
koo•rahz•meh•nohs tired
κουστούμι koos•too•mee
men's suit
κουταλάκι koo•tah•lah•kee
teaspoon
κουτάλι koo•tah•lee n spoon
κουτί koo•tee carton
κουτί πρώτων βοηθειών
koo•tee proh•tohn
voh•ee•thee•ohn first-aid kit
κράμπα krahm•bah n cramp
κραγιόν krah•yohn lipstick
κρατώ krah•toh v keep
κρέμα ξυρίσματος kreh•mah
ksee•rees•mah•tohs shaving
cream
κρεμάστρα kreh•mahs•trah
hanger
κρεβάτι kreh•vah•tee bed
κρυολόγημα kree•oh•loh•
yee•mah n cold (flu)
κρύος kree•ohs adj cold
(temperature)

κρύσταλλο kree•stah•loh n
crystal
κύμα kee•mah n wave
κυλικείο kee•lee•kee•oh
snack bar
κυλιόμενες σκάλες kee•lee•
oh•meh nehs skah•lehs
escalator
Κύπρος kee•prohs Cyprus
κύριος kee•ree•ohs main
κωδικός περιοχής
koh•THee•kohs
peh•ree•oh•khees area code
κωπηλασία koh•pee•lah•see•ah
rowing

Λ

λάμπα lahm•bah lamp, light bulb
λάθος lah•thohs error, wrong
λαιμόκοψη leh•moh•koh•psee
neck (shirt)
λαιμός leh•mohs throat
λάστιχο lahs•tee•khoh tire
(tyre BE)
λειτουργία lee•toor•yee•ah n
mass (church)
λεκές leh•kehs n stain
λεξικό leh•ksee•koh dictionary
λεπτό lehp•toh n minute (time)
λεπτός lehp•tohs adj thin
λέω leh•oh tell
λεωφορείο leh•oh•foh•ree•oh
bus
ληστεία lees•tee•ah robbery
λιμάνι lee•mah•nee n harbor
λίμνη leem•nee n lake
λιμνούλα leem•noo•lah n pond
λιγότερο lee•ghoh•teh•roh less
λιπαντικό lee•pahn•dee•koh
lubricant
λιπαρός lee•pah•rohs greasy
(hair, skin)
λιποθυμώ lee•poh•thee•moh
faint
λίρα lee•rah pound (sterling)
λίτρο lee•troh liter

λογαριασμός loh•ghahr•yahz•mohs n check (bill), account
λοσιόν loh•siohn lotion
λοσιόν μαυρίσματος loh•siohn mahv•rees•mah•tohs sun tan lotion
λουκέτο loo•keh•toh padlock
λουλούδι loo•loo•THee n flower
λουρί ρολογιού loo•ree roh•loh•yioo watch strap
λόφος loh•fohs hill

M

μαγιό mah•yoh swimming trunks, swimsuit
μαθαίνω mah•theh•noh learn
μάθημα ξένης γλώσσας mah•thee mah kseh•nees ghloh•sahs language course
μακιγιάζ mah•kee•yahz make-up
μακριά mahk•ree•ah adv far
μακρύς mak•rees adj long
μαλλιά mah•liah hair
μανικιούρ mah•nee•kioor manicure
μαξιλαροθήκη mah•ksee•lah•roh•thee•kee pillow case
μαργαριτάρι mahr•ghah•ree•tah•ree pearl
μάρτυρας mahr•tee•rahs witness
μας mahs our
μασάζ mah•sahz n massage
μάσκα mahs•kah n mask (diving)
μάτι mah•tee n eye
μαχαίρι mah•kheh•ree knife
με meh with
με άμμο meh ah•moh sandy (beach)
με υπότιτλους meh ee•poh•teet•loos subtitled
με χαλίκια meh khah•lee•kiah pebbly (beach)
μεγαλοπρεπής meh•ghah•lohp•reh•pees magnificent
μεγάλος meh•ghah•lohs adj big, large

μέγεθος meh•yeh•thohs n size
μέδουσα meh•THoo•sah jellyfish
μένω meh•noh v stay
μεριά mehr•yah side (of road)
μερίδα meh•ree•THah n portion
μερικές φορές meh•ree•kehs foh•rehs sometimes
μέσα meh•sah inside
μεσημεριανό meh•see•mehr•yah•noh n lunch
μετά meh•tah after
μετακομίζω meh•tah•koh•mee•zoh v move (room)
μέταλλο meh•tah•loh n metal
μετάξι meh•tah•ksee silk
μεταφέρω meh•tah•feh•roh transfer
μεταφορά meh•tah•foh•rah n transit
μεταφράζω meh•tah•frah•zoh translate
μετάφραση meh•tah•frah•see translation
μεταφραστής meh•tah•frah•stees translator
μέτρηση meh•tree•see measurement
μετρητά meht•ree•tah n cash
μετρό meh•troh subway
μετρώ meht•roh v measure
μη καπνίζοντες mee kap•nee•zon•des non-smoking
μήκος mee•kohs length
μήνας του μέλιτος mee•nahs too meh•lee•tohs honeymoon
μήνυμα mee•nee•mah n message
μηχανή mee•khah•nee engine
μια φορά miah foh•rah once
μικρός meek•rohs little, small
μιλώ mee•loh speak
μίνι-μπαρ mee•nee bahr mini-bar
μισός mee•sohs half
μνημείο mnee•mee•oh memorial, monument

μολυσμένος moh•leez•meh•nohs infected
μονάδα moh•nah•THah unit
μοναδικός moh•nah•THee•kohs unique
μονόκλινο δωμάτιο moh•noh•klee•noh THoh•mah•tee•oh single room
μονοπάτι moh•noh•pah•tee path, trail
μοντέρνος moh•deh•rnohs modern
μοτοποδήλατο moh•toh•poh•THee•lah•toh moped
μουσείο moo•see•oh museum
μουσική moo•see•kee music
μουσικός moo•see•kohs musician
μουστάκι moos•tah•kee moustache
μπαγιάτικος bah•yah•tee•kohs stale
μπάνιο bah•nioh bathroom, lavatory
μπαρ bahr bar
μπάσκετ bah•skeht basketball
μπαστούνια του σκι bahs•too•niah too skee ski poles
μπαταρία bah•tah•ree•ah battery
μπέιμπι σίτερ beh•ee•bee see•tehr babysitter
μπικίνι bee•kee•nee bikini
μπλούζα bloo•zah blouse
μπλουζάκι bloo•zah•kee T-shirt
μπλου-τζην bloo•jeen jeans
μποξ bohks n boxing
μπότα boh•tah boot
μπότες πεζοπορίας boh•tehs peh•zoh•poh•ree•ahs walking boots
μπότες του σκι boh•tehs too skee ski boots
μπουκάλι boo•kah•lee bottle
μπρελόκ breh•lohk key ring

μύγα _mee•ghah_ n fly (insect)
μυρίζω _mee•ree•zoh_ v smell
μυς _mees_ n muscle
μύτη _mee•tee_ n nose
μύωπας _mee•oh•pahs_ short-sighted [BE]
μωρό _moh•roh_ baby

N

ναός _nah•ohs_ temple
ναυαγοσώστης _nah•vah•ghoh•sohs•tees_ lifeguard
ναυαγοσωτική λέμβος _nah•vah•ghoh•sohs•tee•kee lehm•vohs_ lifeboat
ναυτία _nahf•tee•ah_ nausea, travel sickness
νέος _neh•ohs_ young
νερό _neh•roh_ n water
νεύρο _nehv•roh_ nerve
νεφρό _nehf•roh_ kidney
νιπτήρας _nee•ptee•rahs_ sink (bathroom)
νόμιμος _noh•mee•mohs_ legal
νομίζω _noh•mee•zoh_ think
νόμισμα _noh•meez•mah_ currency
νοικιάζω _nee•kiah•zoh_ v hire, rent
νοσοκόμα _noh•soh•koh•mah_ n nurse
νοσοκομείο _noh•soh•koh•mee•oh_ hospital
νόστιμος _nohs•tee•mohs_ delicious
Νοτιοαφρικανός _noh•tee•oh•ahf•ree•kah•nohs_ South African (nationality)
νότιος _noh•tee•ohs_ adj south
ντεμοντέ _deh•mohn•deh_ old-fashioned
ντήζελ _dee•zehl_ diesel
ντους _dooz_ n shower
ντουζίνα _doo•zee•nah_ dozen
νύχι _nee•khee_ n nail
νύχτα _neekh•tah_ night

νυχτερινό κέντρο _neekh•teh•ree•noh kehn•droh_ night club
νωρίς _noh•rees_ early

Ξ

ξαπλώνω _ksah•ploh•noh_ lie down
ξενάγηση _kseh•nah•yee•see_ guided tour
ξενάγηση στα αξιοθέατα _kseh•nah•yee•see stah ah•ksee•oh•theh•ah•tah_ sightseeing tour
ξεναγός _kseh•nah•ghohs_ tour guide
ξένο συνάλλαγμα _kseh•noh see•nah•lahgh•mah_ foreign currency
ξενοδοχείο _kseh•noh•THoh•khee•oh_ hotel
ξένος _kseh•nohs_ foreign
ξενώνας νεότητας _kseh•noh•nahs neh•oh•tee•tahs_ youth hostel
ξεχνώ _ksehkh•noh_ forget
ξεχωριστά _kseh•khoh•ree•stah_ separately
ξινός _ksee•nohs_ sour
ξοδεύω _ksoh•THeh•voh_ v spend
ξύλο _ksee•loh_ wood (material)
ξυπνώ _kseep•noh_ v wake
ξυραφάκι _ksee•rah•fah•kee_ razor, razor blade

Ο

ομάδα _oh•mah•THah_ n team
όμορφος _oh•mohr•fohs_ adj beautiful, pretty
ομπρέλλα _ohm•breh•lah_ sun shade
οβάλ _oh•vahl_ oval
οδηγία _oh•THee•yee•ah_ instruction
οδηγός καταστήματος _oh•THee•ghohs kah•tahs•tee•mah•tohs_ store guide

οδηγός ψυχαγωγίας _oh•THee•ghohs psee•khah•ghoh•yee•ahs_ entertainment guide
οδηγώ _oh•THee•ghoh_ v drive
οδική βοήθεια _oh•THee•kee voh•ee•thee•ah_ road assistance
οδοντίατρος _oh•THohn•dee•ah•trohs_ dentist
οδοντόβουρτσα _oh•THohn•doh•voor•tsah_ tooth brush
οδοντόπαστα _oh•THohn•doh•pahs•tah_ tooth paste
οικογένεια _ee•koh•yeh•nee•ah_ family
οινοποιείο _ee•noh•pee•ee•oh_ winery
όνομα _oh•noh•mah_ n name
όπερα _oh•peh•rah_ opera
οπωροπωλείο _oh•poh•roh•poh•lee•oh_ greengrocer [BE]
οργανωμένος _ohr•ghah•noh•meh•nohs_ organized
ορχήστρα _ohr•khees•trah_ orchestra
οτιδήποτε _oh•tee•THee•poh•teh_ anything
οτοστόπ _oh•toh•stohp_ hitchhiking
οφείλω _oh•fee•loh_ have to (obligation)
οφθαλμίατρος _ohf•thahl•mee•aht•rohs_ optician

Π

παγοπέδιλα _pah•ghoh•peh•THee•lah_ skates
πάγος _pah•ghohs_ n ice
παιδική χαρά _peh•THee•kee khah•rah_ playground
παιδικό κρεβάτι _peh•THee•koh kreh•vah•tee_ crib [cot BE]
παίζω _peh•zoh_ v play (games, music)
παιχνίδι _pehkh•nee•THee_ n game (toy), round

παιχνίδι βίντεο pehkh•_nee_•THee vee•_deh_•oh video game

πακέτο pah•_keh_•toh parcel

πακέτο για το σπίτι pah•_keh_•toh yah toh spee•tee take away

παλιά πόλη pah•_liah_ poh•lee old town

παλιός pah•_liohs_ old (thing)

πάνα μωρού pah•nah moh•_roo_ diaper

Πανεπιστήμιο pah•neh•pees•_tee_•mee•oh university

πάνες μωρού pah•nehs moh•_roo_ nappies

πανόραμα pah•_noh_•rah•mah panorama

παντελόνι pahn•deh•_loh_•nee pants [trousers BE]

παντοπωλείο pahn•doh•poh•_lee_•oh minimart

παντόφλες pahn•_dohf_•lehs slippers

παντρεμένος pahn•dreh•_meh_•nohs married

πάνω pah•noh adj top, upper (berth)

παπούτσι pah•_poo_•tsee shoe

πάρα πολύ pah•rah poh•lee too (extreme)

παραγγέλνω pah•rah•gehl•noh v order

παράδειγμα pah•_rah_•THeegh•mah example

παραδοσιακός pah•rah•THoh•see•ah•_kohs_ traditional

παράθυρο pah•_rah_•thee•roh window

παραλαβή αποσκευών pah•rah•lah•_vee_ ah•poh• skeh•_vohn_ baggage [BE] claim

παραλία pah•rah•_lee_•ah beach

παραλία γυμνιστών pah•rah•_lee_•ah yeem•nees•_tohn_ nudist beach

παραλυσία pah•rah•lee•_see_•ah paralysis

παράνομος pah•_rah_•noh•mohs illegal

παράξενος pah•_rah_•kseh•nohs strange

παραπάνω pah•rah•_pah_•noh more

παρεξήγηση pah•reh•_ksee_• yee•see misunderstanding

πάρκο _pahr_•koh n park

παρκόμετρο pahr•_koh_•meht•roh parking meter

πάρτυ _pahr_•tee n party (social gathering)

παυσίπονο pahf•_see_•poh•noh painkiller

παχύς pah•_khees_ adj fat (person)

πέδιλα peh•THee•lah sandals

πεζόδρομος peh•_zohTH_•roh•mohs pedestrian zone

περιμένω peh•ree•_meh_•noh v hold on, wait

περιμένω στην ουρά peh•ree•_meh_•noh steen oo•_rah_ v queue [BE]

περιέχω peh•ree•_eh_•khoh contain

περιοδικό peh•ree•oh•THee•_koh_ magazine

περίοδος peh•_ree_•oh•THohs period (menstrual)

περιοχή peh•ree•oh•_khee_ region

περιοχή για καπνίζοντες peh•ree•oh•_khee_ yah kahp• _nee_•zohn•dehs smoking area

περιοχή για πικνίκ peh•ree•oh•_khee_ yah peek neek picnic area

περίπτερο peh•_ree_•pteh•roh newsstand, kiosk

περνώ pehr•_noh_ v pass

περπατώ pehr•pah•_toh_ v walk

περσίδες peh•_rsee_•THehs blinds

πετάω peh•_tah_•oh v fly

πετσέτα peh•_tseh_•tah napkin

πέφτω _pehf_•toh v fall

πηγαίνω pee•_yeh_•noh go

πιάτσα ταξί _piah_•tsah tah•_ksee_ taxi rank [BE]

πίεση pee•eh•see blood pressure

πιθανός pee•thah•_nohs_ possible

πινακίδα pee•nah•_kee_•THah road sign

πίνω _pee_•noh v drink

πίπα _pee_•pah pipe (smoking)

πιπίλα pee•_pee_•lah pacifier [soother BE]

πισίνα pee•_see_•nah swimming pool

πιστοποιητικό ασφάλειας pees•toh•pee•ee•tee•_koh_ ahs•_fah_•lee•ahs insurance certificate

πιστωτική κάρτα pees•toh• kee kahr•tah credit card

πιτσαρία pee•tsah•_ree_•ah pizzeria

πλαγιά plah•_yah_ slope (ski)

πλαστική σακούλα plahs•tee•_kee_ sah•_koo_•lah plastic bag

πλατίνα plah•_tee_•nah platinum

πλευρό plehv•_roh_ rib

πλημμύρα plee•_mee_•rah n flood

πληγή plee•_yee_ wound (cut)

πληροφορίες plee•roh•foh•_ree_•ehs information

πληρωμή plee•roh•_mee_ payment

πληρώνω plee•_roh_•noh v pay

πλοίο _plee_•oh n ship

πλυντήριο pleen•_deer_•ee•oh washing machine

πνεύμονας _pnehv_•moh•nahs lung

πόμολο _poh_•moh•loh n handle

ποδήλατο poh•_THee_•lah•toh bicycle

πόδι _poh_•THee foot, leg

ποδόσφαιρο poh•_THohs_•feh•roh soccer [football BE]

ποιότητα *pee•oh•tee•tah* quality

πόλη *poh•lee* town

πολυκατάστημα *poh•lee•kah•tahs•tee•mah* department store

πολυτέλεια *poh•lee•teh•lee•ah* luxury

πολύτιμος *poh•lee•tee•mohs* valuable

πονόδοντος *poh•noh•THohn•dohs* toothache

πονοκέφαλος *poh•noh•keh•fah•lohs* headache

πονόλαιμος *poh•noh•leh•mohs* sore throat

πόνος *poh•nohs* n pain

πόνος στο αυτί *poh•nohs stoh ahf•tee* earache

πόρτα *pohr•tah* door

πορτοφόλι *pohr•toh•foh•lee* wallet

ποσό *poh•soh* n amount

ποσότητα *poh•soh•tee•tah* quantity

ποταμός *poh•tah•mohs* river

ποτέ *poh•teh* never

ποτήρι *poh•tee•ree* glass (container)

ποτό *poh•toh* n drink

πουκάμισο *poo•kah•mee•soh* shirt

πράσινος *prah•see•nohs* green

πρέπει *preh•pee* v must

πρεσβεία *prehz•vee•ah* embassy

πρεσβύωπας *prehz•vee•oh•pahs* long-sighted [BE]

πρήξιμο *pree•ksee•moh* swelling

πρησμένος *preez•meh•nohs* swollen

πρίζα *pree•zah* n plug, socket

πριν *preen* before

πρόβλεψη *prohv•leh•psee* n forecast

πρόβλεψη καιρού *prohv•leh•psee keh•roo* weather forecast

πρόβλημα *prohv•lee•mah* problem

πρόγραμμα *prohgh•rah•mah* n program

πρόγραμμα θεαμάτων *proh•ghrah•mah theh•ah•mah•tohn* program of events

προς *prohs* towards

προσαρμοστής *proh•sahr•moh•stees* adaptor

πρόσβαση *prohz•vah•see* n access

προσγειώνομαι *prohz•yee•oh•noh•meh* v land

προσκαλώ *prohs•kah•loh* v invite

πρόσκληση *prohs•klee•see* invitation

πρόστιμο *prohs•tee•moh* n fine (penalty)

πρόσωπο *proh•soh•poh* n face

προσωρινός *proh•soh•ree•nohs* temporary

προτείνω *proh•tee•noh* suggest

προφέρω *proh•feh•roh* pronounce

προφυλακτικό *proh•fee•lah•ktee•koh* condom

προωθώ *proh•oh•thoh* forward

πρωί *proh•ee* morning

πρωινό *proh•ee•noh* breakfast

πρώτη θέση *proh•tee theh•see* first class

πτήση *ptee•see* flight

πυρετός *pee•reh•tohs* fever

πυροσβεστήρας *pee•rohz•vehs•tee•rahs* fire extinguisher

πυροσβεστική *pee•rohz•vehs•tee•kee* fire brigade [BE]

πυτζάμες *pee•jah•mehs* pajamas

Ρ

ραδιόφωνο *rah•THee•oh•foh•noh* n radio

ρακέτα *rah•keh•tah* racket (tennis, squash)

ραντεβού *rahn•deh•voo* appointment

ράφι *rah•fee* n shelf

ρεματιά *reh•mah•tiah* ravine

ρεσεψιόν *reh•seh•psiohn* reception (hotel)

ρεύμα ποταμού *rehv•mah poh•tah•moo* rapids

ρηχή πισίνα *ree•khee pee•see•nah* paddling pool

ρομαντικός *roh•mahn•dee•kohs* romantic

ρολόι *roh•loh•ee* n watch

ρυάκι *ree•ah•kee* n stream

Σ

σμαράγδι *zmah•ragh•THee* emerald

σαμπουάν *sahm•poo•ahn* n shampoo

σαγιονάρες *sah•yoh•nah•rehs* flip-flops

σαγόνι *sah•ghoh•nee* jaw

σάκκος *sah•kohs* knapsack

σαλόνι *sah•loh•nee* living room

σάουνα *sah•oo•nah* sauna

σαπούνι *sah•poo•nee* n soap

σατέν *sah•tehn* satin

σβήνω *svee•noh* v turn off

σβώλος *svoh•lohs* n lump

σεζ-λονγκ *sehz lohng* deck chair

σενιάν *seh•niahn* rare (steak)

σερβιέτες *sehr•vee•eh•tehs* sanitary towels

σεσουάρ *seh•soo•ahr* hair dryer

σήμα *see•mah* sign (road)

σημαία *see•meh•ah* n flag

σημαίνω *see•meh•noh* v mean

σημείο *see•mee•oh* n point

σίδερο *see•THeh•roh* n iron

σιδερώνω *see•THeh•roh•noh* v
iron, press

σιδηροδρομικός σταθμός
*see•THee•rohTH•roh•mee•
kohs* stahth•*mohs* rail station

σκάλα *skah•lah* ladder

σκάλες *skah•lehs* stairs

σκηνή *skee•nee* tent

σκι *skee* skiing

σκιά *skee•ah* shade (darkness)

σκοπός *skoh•pohs* purpose

σκούπα *skoo•pah* n broom

σκουπίδια *skoo•peeTH•yah* trash
[rubbish BE]

σκούρος *skoo•rohs* adj dark
(color)

σλιπ *sleep* briefs

σόλα *soh•lah* sole (shoes)

σορτς *sohrts* n shorts

σουβενίρ *soo•veh•neer* souvenir

σουπερμάρκετ *soo•pehr•
mahr•keht* supermarket

σουτιέν *soo•tiehn* bra

σπα *spah* spa

σπάγγος *spah•gohs* n string (cord)

σπάνιος *spah•nee•ohs* rare
(unusual)

σπασμένος *spahz•meh•nohs*
broken

σπάω *spah•oh* v break

σπήλαιο *spee•leh•oh* n cave

σπίρτο *speer•toh* n match (to
start fire)

σπονδυλική στήλη
spohn•THee•lee•kee stee•lee
spine

σπουδάζω *spoo•THah•zoh*
v study

σταματώ *stah•mah•toh* v stop

στάδιο *stah•THee•oh* stadium

σταθμός μετρό stahth•*mohs*
meh•troh subway [underground
BE] station

σταθμός λεωφορείων stahTH•
mohs leh•oh•foh•*ree•ohn*
bus station

στάση *stah•see* exposure
(photos), stop (bus)

στάση λεωφορείου *stah•see*
leh•oh•foh•*ree•*oo bus stop

στέγη *steh•yee* n roof

στέλνω *stehl•noh* send

στενός *steh•nohs* adj narrow,
tight

στήθος *stee•*THohs breast

στόμα *stoh•mah* n mouth

στομάχι *stoh•mah•khee* n
stomach

στομαχόπονος *stoh•mah•khoh•
poh•nohs* stomach ache

στολή *stoh•lee* n uniform

στολή δύτη *stoh•lee THee•tee*
wetsuit

στρογγυλός *strohn•gkee•lohs*
adj round

στυλ *steel* n style

στυλό *stee•loh* n pen

συμπεριλαμβάνεται
*seem•beh•ree•lahm•vah•
neh•teh* included

σύζυγος *see•zee•ghohs*
husband, wife

συκώτι *see•koh•tee* liver

σύμπτωμα *seem•ptoh•mah*
symptom

συναγερμός πυρκαγιάς
see•nah•yehr•mohs
peer•kah•yahs* fire alarm

συναντώ *see•nah•noh* meet

συνέδριο *see•neh•THree•oh*
conference

συνταγή γιατρού seen•dah•*yee*
yaht•*roo* prescription

συνταγογραφώ seen•dah•
ghoh•ghrah•*foh* prescribe

συνταξιούχος seen•dah•
ksee•*oo•*khohs retired

σύντομα *seen•doh•mah* soon

συντριβάνι seen•dree•*vah•*nee
fountain

συστάσεις *see•stah•sees*
introductions

συστήνω *see•stee•noh*
introduce, recommend

συχνός seekh•*nohs* adj frequent

σφηνωμένος sfee•noh•
meh•nohs jammed

σφράγισμα *sfrah•yeez•mah*
filling (dental)

σφυρί sfee•*ree* hammer

σχέδιο skheh•THee•oh n plan

σχήμα skhee•mah n shape

σχισμένος skheez•meh•nohs
torn

σχοινί skhee•*nee* n rope

σχολή σκι skhoh•*lee* skee ski
school

σωσίβιο soh•*see•vee•oh*
lifejacket

σωστός sohs•*stohs* adj right
(correct)

Τ

ταμπόν tahm•*bohn* tampon

τάβλι *tah•vlee* backgammon

ταγιέρ tah•*yehr* women's suit

ταΐζω *tah•ee•zoh* v feed

ταινία teh•*nee•ah* n movie

ταξί tah•*ksee* taxi

ταξίδι tah•*ksee•*THee journey

ταξίδι με πλοίο tah•*ksee•*THee
meh plee•oh boat trip

ταξιδιωτική επιταγή
tah•ksee•THee•oh•tee•*kee*
eh•pee•tah•*yee* traveler's
check [traveller's cheque BE]

ταξιδιωτικό γραφείο
tah•ksee•THyoh•tee•*koh*
ghrah•*fee•*oh travel agency

ταξιτζής tah•ksee•*jees* taxi
driver

ταυτότητα tahf•*toh•*tee•tah
identification

ταχυδρομείο tah•kheeTH•
roh•mee•oh post office

ταχυδρομική επιταγή
tah•kheeTH•roh•mee•*kee*
eh•pee•tah•*yee* money order

ταχυδρομικό κουτί
*tah•khee TH•roh•mee•koh
koo•tee* mailbox [postbox BE]

τεμάχιο *teh•mah•khee•oh*
piece

τελειώνω *teh•lee•oh•noh v* end

τελευταί ος *teh•lehf•teh•ohs*
last

τελεφερίκ *teh•leh•feh•reek*
cablecar

τέλος *teh•lohs n* end

τελωνειακή δήλωση
*teh•loh•nee•ah•kee
THeh•loh•see* customs declaration (tolls)

τελωνείο *teh•loh•nee•oh*
customs (tolls)

τέννις *teh•nees* tennis

τετράγωνος *teht•rah•ghoh•
nohs* square

τζετ-σκι *jeht skee* jet-ski

τζόγκινγκ *joh•geeng* jogging

τζόγος *joh•ghohs* gambling

τηλεκάρτα *tee•leh•kahr•tah*
phone card

τηλεόραση *tee•leh•oh•rah•see*
TV

τηλεφώνημα *tee•leh•
foh•nee•mah* phone call

τηλεφωνικός θάλαμος
*tee•leh•foh•nee•kohs thah•
lah•mohs* telephone booth

τηλεφωνικός κατάλογος *tee•
leh•foh•nee•kohs kah•tah•
loh•ghohs* telephone directory

τηλέφωνο *tee•leh•foh•noh*
n phone

την *teen* per

τιμή συναλλάγματος *tee•mee
see•nah•lahgh•mah•tohs*
exchange rate

τιμή εισόδου *tee•mee
ee•soh•THoo* entrance fee

τιρμπουσόν *teer•boo•sohn*
corkscrew

τοίχος *tee•khohs* wall

τοπικός *toh•pee•kohs* local

τοστιέρα *toh•stieh•rah* toaster

τουαλέτα *too•ah•leh•tah*
restroom (toilet BE)

τούνελ *too•nehl* tunnel

τουρίστας *too•rees•tahs* tourist

τουριστική θέση *too•rees•
kee theh•see* economy class

τουριστικός οδηγός *too•ree•
stee•kohs oh•THee•ghohs*
guide book

τραβώ το καζανάκι *trah•voh toh
kah•zah•nah•kee* flush

τραμ *trahm* tram

τράπεζα *trah•peh•zah* bank

τραπέζι *trah•peh•zee* table

τραπεζομάντηλο *trah•peh•
zoh•mahn•dee•loh* tablecloth

τραυματισμένος *trahv•mah•
teez•meh•nohs* injured

τρένο *treh•noh* train

τρέχω *treh•khoh v* run, speed

τρόμπα *trohm•bah n* pump

τρόλλεϋ *troh•leh•ee* trolley-bus

τρύπα *tree•pah* hole (in clothes)

τρώω *troh•oh* eat

τσάντα *tsahn•dah* handbag

τσίμπημα *tsee•bee•mah n* bite,
sting (insect)

τσίμπημα κουνουπιού
tseem•bee•mah koo•noo•piooh
mosquito bite

τυπικός *tee•pee•kohs* typical

τύχη *tee•khee* luck

Υ

υγρό πιάτων *eegh•roh piah•tohn*
dishwashing detergent

υπεραστικό λεωφορείο
*ee•peh•rahs•tee•koh
leh•oh•foh•ree•oh* long-
distance bus

υπεραστικό τηλεφώνημα
*ee•peh•ahs•tee•koh
tee•leh•foh•nee•mah* long-
distance call

υπέρβαρο *ee•pehr•vah•roh*
excess baggage [BE]

υπηκοότητα
ee•pee•koh•oh•tee•tah
nationality

υπηρεσία *ee•pee•reh•see•ah
n* service (administration,
business)

υπηρεσία δωματίου
*ee•pee•reh•see•ah
THoh•mah•tee•oo* room service

υπηρεσία πλυντηρίου
*ee•pee•reh•see•ah
pleen•dee•ree•oo* laundry
service

υπνόσακκος *ee•pnoh•sah•kohs*
sleeping bag

υπνωτικό χάπι
eep•noh•tee•koh khah•pee
sleeping pill

υπόγειος *ee•poh•ghee•ohs*
underground [BE]

υπολογιστής
ee•poh•loh•yee•stees
computer

υπόνομος *ee•poh•noh•mohs*
sewer

ύφασμα *ee•fahs•mah* fabric
(cloth)

ύψος *ee•psohs* height

Φ

φακός *fah•kohs* flashlight, lens

φακός επαφής *fah•kohs
eh•pah•fees* contact lens

υπηρεσία φαξ
ee•pee•reh•see•ah fahks
fax facility

φάρμα *fahr•mah n* farm

φάρμακο *fahr•mah•kah*
medication

φαρδύς *fahr•THees* loose
(fitting), wide

φάρος *fah•rohs* lighthouse

φέρνω *fehr•noh* bring

φέρυ-μπωτ *feh•ree boht* ferry

φεστιβάλ fehs•tee•_vahl_ festival

φεύγω fehv•ghoh v leave (depart)

φιλμ feelm n film (camera)

φίλη fee•lee girlfriend

φιλί fee•_lee_ n kiss

φιλοδώρημα fee•loh•THoh•ree•mah gratuity

φίλος fee•lohs friend, boyfriend

φίλτρο feel•troh n filter

φιλώ fee•_loh_ v kiss

φλέβα fleh•vah vein

φλεγμονή flegh•moh•_nee_ inflammation

φλυτζάνι flee•_jah_•nee cup

φοβερός foh•veh•_rohs_ terrible

φοβισμένος foh•veez•_meh_•nohs frightened

φοιτητής fee•tee•_tees_ student

φόρεμα foh•reh•mah n dress

φόρος foh•rohs duty (customs), tax

φορώ foh•_roh_ v wear

φούρνος foor•nohs oven

φούρνος μικροκυμάτων foor•nohs mee•kroh•kee•_mah_•tohn microwave (oven)

φούστα foo•stah skirt

φούτερ foo•tehr sweatshirt

ΦΠΑ fee•pee•_ah_ sales tax

φράγμα frahgh•mah n lock (river, canal)

φράση frah•see n phrase

φράχτης frahkh•tees n fence

φρέσκος frehs•kohs adj fresh

φτάνω ftah•noh arrive

φτηνός ftee•_nohs_ cheap, inexpensive

φτιάχνω τις βαλίτσες ftee•_ahkh_•noh tees vah•_lee_•tsehs v pack (baggage)

φυλακή fee•lah•_kee_ n prison

φύση fee•see nature

φυτό fee•_toh_ n plant

φως fohs n light (electric)

φώτα foh•tah lights (car)

φωτογραφία foh•tohgh•rah•_fee_•ah v photo

φωτογραφική μηχανή foh•tohgh•rah•fee•_kee_ mee•khah•_nee_ camera

φωτοτυπικό foh•toh•tee•pee•_koh_ photocopier

Χ

χαμηλώνω khah•mee•_loh_•noh v turn down (volume, heat)

χαλί khah•_lee_ rug

χαλκός khahl•_kohs_ copper

χάπι khah•pee tablet

χάρτης khahr•tees n map

χαρτί khar•_tee_ paper

χαρτί κουζίνας khah•_rtee_ koo•_zee_•nahs kitchen

χαρτί υγείας khahr•_tee_ ee•_yee_•ahs toilet paper

χαρτομάντηλο khahr•toh•_mahn_•dee•loh tissue

χαρτομάντηλο khahr•toh•_mahn_•dee•loh handkerchief

χείλη khee•lee lips

χειροκίνητος khee•roh•_kee_•nee•tohs manual (car)

χειρότερος khee•_roh_•teh•rohs worse

χιλιόμετρα khee•_lioh_•meh•trah mileage

χιονίζει khioh•_nee_•zee v snow

χλιαρός khlee•ah•_rohs_ lukewarm

χόμπυ khoh•bee hobby (pastime)

χοντρός khohn•_drohs_ thick

χορεύω khoh•_reh_•voh v dance

χορτοφάγος khohr•toh•_fah_•ghohs vegetarian

χρειάζομαι khree•_ah_•zoh•meh v need

χρέωση υπηρεσίας _khreh_•oh•see ee•pee•reh•_see_•ahs service charge

χρήματα _khree_•mah•tah money

χρησιμοποιώ khree•see•moh•pee•_oh_ v use

χρήσιμος _khree_•see•mohs useful

χρονική περίοδος khroh•nee•_kee_ peh•_ree_•oh•THohs period (time)

χρυσός khree•_sohs_ n gold

χρώμα _khroh_•mah n color

χρωστώ khroh•_stoh_ owe

χτένα _khteh_•nah n comb

χτενίζω khteh•_nee_•zoh v comb

χτες khtehs yesterday

χώρα _khoh_•rah country (nation)

χωριό khohr•_yoh_ village

χωρίς khoh•rees without

χώρος _khoh_•rohs n space (area)

χώρος κάμπινγκ _kah_•mpeeng _khoh_•rohs campsite

χώρος στάθμευσης _khoh_•rohs _stahth_•mehf•sees car park (BE)

χώρος στάθμευσης _khoh_•rohs _stahth_•mehf•sees parking lot

Ψ

ψαλίδι psah•_lee_•THee scissors

ψάρεμα _psah_•reh•mah fishing

ψάχνω _psahkh_•noh look for

ψηλός psee•_lohs_ tall

ψύλλος _psee_•lohs flea

Ω

ώμος _oh_•mohs n shoulder (anatomy)

ώρα αιχμής _oh_•rah ehkh•_mees_ rush hour

ώρες λειτουργίας _oh_•rehs lee•toor•_yee_•ahs opening hours

INDEX

Berlitz pocket guide

ZÁKYNTHOS AND KEFALONIÁ

Fifth Edition 2020

Editors: Carine Tracanelli, Sian Marsh
Authors: Nick Edwards, Maria Lord
Head of DTP and Pre-Press: Rebeka Davies
Layout: Aga Bylica
Managing Editor: Carine Tracanelli
Picture Editors: Tom Smyth, Aude Vauconsant
Cartography Update: Carte
Photography Credits: Alamy 4MC, 4ML,
43, 46, 53, 87; Bigstock 7R, 29; Britta
Jaschinski/Apa Publications 93, 103;
Cephalonia Botanica 59; Dreamstime 21;
Fotolia 97; Getty Images 1, 5MC, 83, 84,
91; iStock 4TL, 5T, 5TC, 5M, 5M, 16, 26,
35, 41, 48, 50, 58, 66, 67, 78, 79, 80, 82, 98;
Kevin Cummins/Apa Publications 11, 14,
24, 55, 56, 64, 68, 71, 72, 74, 77, 89, 94, 100;
Mockford & Bonnetti/Apa Publications 30,
61; Shutterstock 4TC, 5MC, 6L, 6R, 7, 13, 19,
23, 33, 37, 39, 44, 60, 62
Cover Picture: Shutterstock

Distribution
UK, Ireland and Europe: Apa Publications
(UK) Ltd; sales@insightguides.com
United States and Canada: Ingram
Publisher Services; ips@ingramcontent.com
Australia and New Zealand: Woodslane;
info@woodslane.com.au
Southeast Asia: Apa Publications (SN) Pte;
singaporeoffice@insightguides.com
Worldwide: Apa Publications (UK) Ltd;
sales@insightguides.com

**Special Sales, Content Licensing
and CoPublishing**
Insight Guides can be purchased in bulk
quantities at discounted prices. We can
create special editions, personalised jackets
and corporate imprints tailored to your
needs. sales@insightguides.com;
www.insightguides.biz

All Rights Reserved
© 2020 Apa Digital (CH) AG and
Apa Publications (UK) Ltd

Printed in Poland by Interak

Contact us
Every effort has been made to provide
accurate information in this publication,
but changes are inevitable. The publisher
cannot be responsible for any resulting loss,
inconvenience or injury. We would appreciate
it if readers would call our attention to any
errors or outdated information. We also
welcome your suggestions; please contact
us at: berlitz@apaguide.co.uk
www.insightguides.com/berlitz

Berlitz Trademark Reg. U.S. Patent Office
and other countries. Marca Registrada.
Used under licence from the Berlitz
Investment Corporation